Taming the Wild Child

A Practical Guide to Navigating the Early Years

Taming the Wild Child

A Practical Guide to Navigating the Early Years

Jacalyn Wetzel

MSW, LCSW-A

Taming the Wild Child

A Practical Guide to Navigating the Early Years

Copyright © 2019 Jacalyn Wetzel

All rights reserved. No part of this book may be reproduced in any manner whatsoever, or stored in any information storage system, without the prior written consent of the publisher or the author, except in the case of brief quotations with proper reference, embodied in critical articles and reviews.

Cover and interior design by Jacalyn Wetzel

ISBN: 9781983467899

Disclaimer: This publication is sold with the understanding that the author is not engaged in rendering psychological, medical or other professional services. If expert assistance or counseling is needed, the services of a competent professional should be sought.

DEDICATION

This book is dedicated to all my mamas and daddies out there doing the best they can to raise good humans. I see you. You are doing a great job, and if no one has told you yet today, I'm proud of you. Remember, these are all ages, stages, and phases that will all eventually pass.

1
I'm Screwing it Up

This parenting thing is hard. If you were looking for pretty lies in this book, I'm sorry. I won't be lying to you in any of these chapters. My hope for this book is for it to be a no nonsense, practical parenting book. I want you to leave this book with the understanding that…

1. You are not alone in your struggle. And 2. Your child is not broken.

If you have purchased this book, it's likely because you have a "wild child," are struggling with parenting, or you've been convinced your child is feral and can't be tamed.

Recently, there has been this trend of calling children feral, and throwing your hands up in the air as if to say, "nothing can be done, my child or children are feral." I'm sorry, I know I'm going to hurt some feelings with what I'm about to say, but your children are not feral. They're not. Please stop saying that.

Feral implies that they are some sort of wild animal, and in claiming that title for your child, you're sending yourself and your child the subtle message that behaving in a wild manner is acceptable and can't be changed. Your children are not feral, they are likely lacking consistency in consequences. Is this to say that you're somehow screwing them up, no. You are doing the best you can with what you have. There's nothing wrong with that.

Your child likely won't grow up to be an ax murderer because you allowed them to grow up more feral than their more well-behaved counterparts. Sometimes it's easier to admit that your child is feral, or wild, than it is to admit we have no idea what we are doing. But, why is that?

Did your baby come with a "how to raise a tiny human" manual? My children didn't. I mean, if someone wrote that manual to give out to every new parent at the hospital, and I'm missing my copy, then I'm going to be ticked. Parenting is an on the job training position. We are all perfect parents until we are sent home from the hospital with our tiny, squishy, real life pooping and peeing *Baby Alive* doll.

If you've never had a *Baby Alive* doll as a kid, you were missing out. Just kidding, it was pretty gross. Kind of like real babies. If this were in a text message I'd put a winking and laughing emoji behind that last sentence.

My hope is, that the second paragraph of this book didn't immediately turn you off, because this book is legitimately for you, sweet mama (and daddies). It's for the parents out there struggling, doing the best they can, but still beating themselves up because they feel like their child is feral, or worse, bad.

I actually hate the term bad. Like, honest to goodness, abhor it with every fiber of my being when someone is using it to describe a child, and it sends hair prickling chills down my spine when they are using it to describe *their* child. If you call your child bad, please do yourself and your child a favor and stop it. Please, for the love of all things holy, if you do nothing else that I suggest from this book; stop calling your child bad.

Let me explain. The word bad implies that they are broken. It implies that they themselves are bad children. Bad people. Who likes or, better yet, loves a bad person? The answer is no one. No one loves a bad person, because they're...bad. When you use this negative connotation to describe your child, you are approaching them from a different headspace than you would if they were a "good kid."

So, I challenge you to figure out what is bad about your child's behavior and reframe it, and while we are in the business of reframing it, harness it. Chances are, if your child is "bad," they are something very different.

Your child is persistent, determined, a go getter, a leader, a no nonsense I'm not accepting that answer future CEO.

Do you know what makes future leaders and CEOs? Not accepting no for an answer when doors are closed in their face to whatever their dream may be.

Leaders *are* persistent. Leaders *are* determined. Leaders *are* no nonsense, pull no punches awesome human beings. Don't take that away from your child by calling them "bad." Tell them who they are destined to be. Teach them how to harness that energy and use it for good.

I know you're thinking I'm a crazy lady at this point. I'm not. Stick with me, I promise I'll show you what the heck I'm talking about. Let's say you have a daughter that's bossy. Bossy is another word I despise by the way. Anyway, let's say your daughter is Bossy McBossypants. Instead of viewing her as bossy, we are going to reframe her behavior and say she's direct and delegates well.

How can we harness this behavior? The first thing we want to do is when we see her using her direct delegation skills, we are going to praise her behavior that we like. That looks something like this, "I like that you can tell your friends when you need help." We immediately want to follow that praise with the next sentence, "Can you think of a nicer way to ask for help? They might be more willing to help you if you ask nicely." Now, some experts don't like the term "I like," because it places the emphasis on pleasing the parent and you want their pleasure with themselves to come internally, not externally. So, if you are of that mindset, you can replace that with "You are going to be a great leader one day. Let's think of a way to ask nicely so you can get some help picking up these toys."

Any time we are addressing a child, especially when correcting a behavior, we want to remember to get down on their level so you can look each other in the eye. Think about the last time you were called into your boss's office. Don't have a boss? Think about the last time you and your significant other were having a disagreement. Imagine, if you will, that you were sitting and for whatever reason could not stand up, and they stood fairly close to you while talking down at you with a stern voice.

Does that make you uncomfortable just imagining someone bigger than you hovering over you while you remain seated? Well, children can't suddenly sprout up to meet your gaze while you are working to correct a behavior. Something magical happens to you both when you get down on their level. Your voice softens because you're eighteen inches away from their face. When your voice softens, their resolve softens. You're both in a more relaxed and pliable state. This is where you want to be when you're correcting an unwanted behavior. We want to mold that child to use those strong personality traits for something positive. If you can get down on their level, by stooping and gently holding their hand or placing a gentle hand on their back, you are saying to them in that moment, they matter. They are important, and so is what they are trying to communicate.

Now, you may be reading this and saying, "Great, I've been doing it all wrong." Well, you know what? We all do it all wrong at some point. We are not perfect humans. Even Jesus was a spirited child. No pun intended. But do you think Mary and Joseph knew what to do when Jesus rose his childhood friend from the dead to exonerate him of the accusation that he pushed him off the cliff? To be sure, Mary and Joseph were dumbstruck. Just as you would be. Just as you should be at some points in parenting. You don't have all the answers.

Me, with two fancy degrees, one of which is specifically for child development and family relations, I don't have all the answers. My kids stump me at times. When my friends come to me for advice, there have been times I've had to say, "I have no idea, but let's try this and see what happens."

Not knowing something does not equate to being bad at something. I'm going to say that again for the people in the back.

Not knowing something does not mean you're bad at something.

You know what you do know? You know your child. You know your child better than anyone else knows your child. You know how to love that child in the unique way that that child needs to be loved, and that's powerful. That's something to be proud of, so take a moment and relish in that feeling. If your child is happy, and healthy, and you've picked up this book, you're already ahead of the game.

I'm going to ask you to do something you might think is a little weird. Do it anyway. And no, I'm not being bossy, I'm being direct. I want you to sit down with a pen and paper and write out all the good qualities you love about parenting your child.

Write down all the things you do right. Write down all the ways that you are a good mama or daddy.

Do you have your list? Great! Now take that list and place it somewhere you can see it daily. That place might be your planner, your bedroom wall, or your bathroom mirror. Wherever it is, just make sure you can see it daily, so you can be reminded of how good of a job you are already doing as a parent. You are already kicking parenting butt!

Now, I want you to make another list. Make a list of all the things you think you're lacking as a parent. Do you not play enough? Not bathe them enough? Not make them brush their teeth enough and sometimes they go to school breathing their dragon breath all over everyone within a five-foot radius. Did you make that list? Good. Now, take that list, ball it up and...you guessed it. THROW IT IN THE TRASH where it belongs.

Didn't I just tell you that you were already kicking parenting butt?! I meant that.

Every day that you feel like you have somehow failed your child, I want you to go find that first list we made. Yeah, the one that tells you how awesome of a parent you are. Find that list and read it. Read it until your eyes go blurry, because mama, you are all those things for your child. You are amazing.

Since there is no such thing as a perfect parent, I mean, except for those that have never had children, or raised them, you should know there's always room for growth. That's what this book is about. Growth. I want you to grow as parents. I want your children to grow into good humans. I want to change the world by guiding parents to reach and then exceed their parenting potential.

Yes, that might seem like a strange dream. But, I don't think people understand exactly how passionate I am about parenting. Parenting is my jam.

I love the mess out of parenting. I love helping parents figure this thing out. I love that lightbulb moment that happens when their child's behavior starts changing. It's such a rush for me.

I know, I'm strange, but everyone has their thing. The one thing that calls to their heart and gets their adrenaline pumping overtime. For me it's parenting. It's also watching a child learn to regulate their emotions and behaviors.

I used to work at a childcare center with preschoolers. I came in after a teacher who was not so great with children got fired. This class was the dreaded class of the entire center.

No one wanted to give breaks in this classroom. No one wanted to teach in this classroom. I watched the classroom with envy from a distance and wanted nothing more than to teach those babies.

Then, I got my chance. Within weeks the children were behaved. The child labeled "that kid," was now regulating his own emotions. Every time someone complimented my class, my heart filled with joy.

These children were not bad. This class was not unruly. The kids just needed a healthy balance of love, attention, fun, and consequences. That's it.

I didn't yell at my class. I didn't punish them. Most of the consequences were natural and logical. I gave them responsibilities. I gave them praise. Was it hard? Abso-freaking-lutely it was hard. The first few days it was like herding cats with a fire hose.

But they saw a calm teacher that got down on their level. A teacher that played with them and validated their big feelings. Someone who showed them how to calm down when they couldn't figure it out. I became their safe place. I became someone they could laugh with, and scowl at when I made them mad with my rules. These kids were not bad y'all. These kids were just kids learning to move through the world with all of these grown up expectations placed on them.

So, are you screwing it up? No. You're not. You're not screwing it up because of every good thing you placed on that list. You're not screwing it up because your thirst for growth led you here. You're not screwing it up because you are continuing to seek help. And seeking help means that you're admitting that you don't know everything. Which, of course you don't know everything. No one does. Your child will not remember that one time you forgot to pack a PB&J but put a ham sandwich in his lunch box instead. They won't remember that you once forgot it was wacky tacky day and they were one of the only normally dressed kids at school on a random Wednesday. They won't remember that you forgot to sign their dang Friday folder for three weeks straight because you have three other children that need things signed, you have a big deadline approaching for work and you still have to get the oil changed after taking your daughter to get her braces adjusted. They won't remember. I promise.

Every day that you wake up, you have another day to be awesome. You have another day to give yourself and your children some grace. You have another day to be the best parent that you can be for that day. Some days being the best parent for the day may look like throwing $2 at your kid as they army roll out of your car in car rider lane. And some days being the best parent for the day may look like making a four-course dinner after having time to volunteer in the classroom for three hours.

Whatever the best parenting version of you is on that day, give yourself some grace. We all need it.

2
Little Bodies, Big Emotions

It's not just your child. If you think it's just your child, please get that idea out of your head.

Your child is not the only child that throws a fit in the store because they didn't get what they wanted. Your child is not the only one that refuses to move because you won't let him wear his Batman costume to church. It's not you, and it's not your child. Your precious little chubby cheeked toddler or preschooler is learning to navigate big gigantic emotions that no one has prepared them for.

You think you weren't prepared to be a parent? They weren't prepared to be an emotional being. They were perfectly happy curled up, floating around in our amniotic fluid minding their own business, kick boxing with your spleen. I guarantee you; they were happy. We brought them into this world and placed all of these expectations on them to behave a certain way when they have strong feelings. Feelings that they have never had before. It's our job to teach them how to handle those feelings.

One way they learn is through watching you. Yes, you. They watch everything you do whether you want them to or not. So that time you dropped your pizza and cussed, then kicked the trash can...yeah, they saw that. When I was a kid, my mother used to tell us to "do what I say, not as I do," and this was something I heard repeatedly throughout my childhood. This is not an adage that works, and I'm not sure why it was even started.

In fact, the do what I say and not what I do thought process is why so many parents don't realize that their children are watching and absorbing everything they see them do. Even the things you didn't realize they were watching. You are their model for how a human is supposed to behave, so the first step to raising a good human is to check your own behaviors.

Children are indeed little sponges. The way you spoke to the server last Tuesday, they absorbed that. The way you handled being yelled at by a stranger on your way to drop them off at daycare, they saw that. The thing is, they don't care how other people are behaving at this age. You are their sun, moon and stars. They only care about how their parents are behaving.

If they see you being a good person, using polite words even through anger or hurt feelings, they will follow suit. If they see you blowing up over little things because you had a bad day, they will have a mini explosion when they can't stack their blocks the right way. You are their model of the ideal human. I cannot stress this enough. They learn how to regulate their big emotions by watching their parents regulate theirs.

I have a friend who has trouble with whining from her now early school-ager. This problem has been a consistent issue since her child was a toddler. My friend comes to me often for parenting advice and wondering how to break this whiny and "brat" like behavior. Before anyone gets any ideas, brat is her word, not mine. Anyway, this friend cannot figure out why her child is behaving in this manner when she tries to teach her otherwise.

Do you see where I'm going here? My friend whines. Constantly. I've seen her whine over small things, and big things, and it doesn't bother me because it's part of her personality. Now, don't get me wrong, I absolutely love this person and I am very truthful with what the issue may be, but this is a habit my friend has to break if she wants to see any change in her child's whining.

I mean, whining isn't the end of the world, and for most children it's pretty effective to get the things they want, but in this case, my friend wants to break this behavior. The thing is, my friend is a good mama. Like, a seriously good mama. So, the whining issue is one that can be addressed or left as is because her children are well behaved children and whining doesn't change that. The point of that random story is to say that children do what they see, not what you say.

So, now that we've established the first line of defense to help children manage their feelings, let's move on to another action step. This is a tangible thing you can do this weekend if you have about twenty minutes to spare. I used this when I was teaching preschool, and with my own children. Create a quiet corner for them.

What is a quiet corner you ask? Just what it sounds like. It's a small space in their room, living room, or playroom that is designed with quiet activities in mind. This is a place they can come to regulate their big emotions when they are having a hard time getting themselves together. You will have to train them to use the quiet corner, but once they have it figured out, they will seek the quiet corner instead of throwing an unwanted fit.

They will learn how to cope with their feelings by sitting with them, feeling their feelings and seeking out an adult when they are ready to talk or need a hug to wrap everything up with a bow. Eventually they will get so good at sitting with their emotions before behaving in an unwanted way that they will be able to utilize this technique in public.

How do you make a quiet corner? I'm glad you asked. I'm going to list it out in steps for you, so it makes the most sense, and who doesn't love a list when trying to learn something new.

Quiet Corner Steps

1. Find an area in the house that is child proofed and safe for a child to spend some time alone.
2. In this safe area, be it a playroom or the child's bedroom, find a corner or area of the room that's free from distractions.
3. Place a soft rug on the floor, one that has some texture. Your sense of touch can help calm you.
4. Find a bean bag, or multiple brightly colored pillows and place them on the floor.
5. Don't forget to add the stuffed animals to keep them company.
6. Those books that are scattered around their room, find a bookshelf to hold them. They have some preschool bookshelves on Amazon pretty cheap. Slide that bad boy in

the quiet corner. If you don't have that kind of room, Amazon also has floating bookshelves to hang on the wall.
7. You can paint this corner a calming color, or even paint an area with chalkboard paint so they can draw on the wall while they're calming down. You don't have to paint if you don't want to obviously. Wall decals work just as well, or nothing at all. It's your house.
8. Put a few sensory bottles in the corner as well (we will go over how to make those pretty cheap).
9. If you'd like you can add an easy to turn on sound machine.
10. It's your house. Your child. Find something to make it fit their personality.

You may notice that I only mentioned quiet things to go in the quiet corner. That's because it's a quiet corner. Quiet activities go into the quiet corner because this is where they come to gather their thoughts and emotions. Something very important that I should mention here.

The quiet corner is not for punishment. That's not to say that if your child is having a meltdown that you don't put them in the quiet area, because you do. That's exactly what the quiet corner is for. If your kid is screaming over the cheese stick you gave him, because he wanted grapes, you take them to the quiet area and tell them to find something in that area to do until they can calm down. There is no time limit. It's just a place they can regulate their emotions, and they have control over when they leave the area.

If you are consistent with sending them to the quiet corner in a loving way and explaining they can come out whenever they are feeling better, they will start to put themselves in the quiet area anytime they are feeling upset or overwhelmed.

Be sure to reinforce talking about their feelings after they leave the quiet area, as this helps them process their emotions and get used to the idea of venting to their parents about how they are feeling, so in middle school, and high school, they will still be coming to you to talk about some big issues they may be facing.

Have you ever tried to think, or better yet talk while you, yourself were having big emotions? We all have. It's not pretty. We cry, we stutter, or even worse, we yell and say hurtful things to people we love. Some of us have learned to not speak through these big emotions, but to collect ourselves and our thoughts and revisit it later. This is what we want to teach our children. If more people learned how to regulate their feelings as preschoolers, we would have less instances of road rage and hateful acts that are a direct result of not managing your emotions well.

Not managing your emotions well in front of your child only leads to your child not managing their emotions well either in front of you, or when you're not around at all. If this happens, don't beat yourself up. Apologize.

Apologizing to a child can be a strange and new concept to some people, while to others it may seem like a no brainer. Let me explain the importance of apologizing to your child. Apologizing lets your child know that they are important. It lets them know that their feelings are valued, and adults make mistakes too. Apologizing to your child, also teaching them humility. Taking the time to say "I shouldn't have behaved that way, and I'm sorry" teaches them that if they make a mistake, they too can humbly ask for some grace.

Grace is so important when it comes to parenting, guys. I'm sure I could write a whole chapter on grace. I won't, but I could. Grace is saying to yourself, to your child, and to others, today was just not our day, but I love you and we will try again tomorrow. Grace is so excruciatingly important to healthy child development, and healthy relationship development in general.

Think about the last time someone showed you some grace when you messed up or had a bad day and took it out on someone unsuspecting that didn't deserve it. Didn't it make you feel like everything would be ok? Didn't it make your load feel a little lighter because you didn't have to carry the guilt? Show your babies some grace when they are in the midst of a tantrum.

Things That Help Manage Big Emotions

1. Sensory motivated items. Think of the five senses. Something soft to touch, this could be an old blankie, teddy bear or whatever is their lovey at the time. Sensory bottles (old water bottle filled most of the way with water, a few drops of food coloring, a couple of drops of oil, and some glitter, glue the top on with some Elmer's glue or rubber cement. Voila!), this is something they can see. The movement of the water can help soothe an angry or

dysregulated child. Something they can smell. You can put some lavender essential oils on their favorite lovey or spray it with a little bit of your perfume or body spray. Smelling something familiar can help them come back down to a level where they can explain what is going on. Soothing music or nature sounds are good tools as well. Have them sit quietly and listen if they're in the space to do that. Finally, taste. Sometimes kids are just hangry. Try a healthy snack and talking again after they've eaten.

2. Exercise. Dance parties are always a favorite amongst little ones, and why wouldn't they be. Dance parties are a favorite amongst many adults. So, if your kid is in a sour mood, try the dance it out method. They don't like to dance or don't want to, try to get them to go on a short sprint to the end of the driveway and back to see if they can beat mom or dad. Going to the park is also a good alternative if you have the time in that moment.

3. Affection. Sometimes they just need a hug. Affection allows them to feel their feelings and know that they are in a safe place.

4. Validation. Validate their feelings. Tell them that you understand that they are feeling angry, frustrated or sad. Give their feelings names so later they can tell you what they are feeling and can identify them correctly. Someone took their toy and they start to cry? Tell them you know that it made them sad that someone took their toy, because it would make

you sad if someone took theirs, then help them come up with a way to ask for it back.
5. Distraction. This is usually a good technique with toddlers but can still apply to preschoolers. Distract them with something else. Quickly give a name to their feelings and validate them, then distract them with another object or something else they could be doing besides whatever it is that is causing this big emotion.

These are just some of the steps to help you teach your child to regulate their emotions, but let me tell you, emotions that big take a little while to get a handle on. Teaching children to regulate these big emotions can become a full-time job, but it's so worth it. When we take the time to put in the work when our children are toddlers and preschoolers, we eliminate a lot of the issues that parents face when their children are school-age or older.

Putting in the work is redundant. Putting in the work is frustrating because it doesn't happen fast. This is something you have to work at. Just like your child is having to work at not biting their sister or throwing their *Sofia the First* doll at you when you tell them no, you have to work at teaching them the appropriate way to handle their feelings.

Mama, I know, you have a million and one things on your plate, but I promise you, this...this is worth its weight in gold filled Legos. This will make the years so much smoother.

Emotional regulation is hard to teach adults, I know, I'm a therapist and do it daily. Adults or teens that are emotionally dysregulated cry at the mere mention of a hint of criticism, or they punch holes in walls or respond in some other over the top way to something that would otherwise be a small hiccup in plans.

We've all met emotionally dysregulated people. They're the Karen's yelling at the Walmart bakery person because they don't make Cake Boss-like cakes. They're the Dave's of the world honking their horns red-faced while cursing you to the moon and back because you didn't go when the light turned green .3 seconds ago.

These people we encounter on a regular basis are for whatever reason not able to appropriately regulate their feelings. Teaching your children early to learn how to manage these feelings will only make them better humans in the future.

So, take the time, or better yet, *make* the time to teach your children how to navigate these big emotions in their tiny bodies. The bodies and the emotions only get bigger you guys. They only get harder to manage, because instead of being upset because their Barbie was lost, they're now upset because they lost their job and they can't make rent. We can help them now or they'll be in my office later.

3
Electronics are the Devil

I'm sorry to all of you mamas out there that are glaring at Judy from across the room because she's glaring at your 2-year-old with their tablet propped up on the dinner table, so you can actually shove food in your own mouth. I'm so sorry.

Listen. I. Get. It. I get it! I have four children, yes four. One is only 13 months old and doesn't have any electronics, though he tries to take everyone's phone as soon as they set them down within reach. He's also perfectly happy with an old cable remote without batteries, so it's fairly easy to do the bait and switch. My older boys, 13, and 11, have regulations on their electronic devices. They don't get them all the time. They can *earn* thirty minutes of electronic time during the week.

You absolutely read that correctly. They can earn it. Once they earn it, it is only thirty minutes of time. Why? Because they don't need their phones. They pay exactly zero bills. They have a combined number of zero wives, and zero children, so who is it that they would desperately need to get into contact with? The answer is no one.

When we were younger, our phones were the family phone in the kitchen or living room, and we all survived, and thrived. Kids do not need phones glued to their hands starting at age four. They just don't. It's simply not healthy, and we will get into the why a little later in this chapter.

Now, you may think I'm only talking about their phones, but I'm talking about all electronics. Their laptops, tablets, and gaming computer are all regulated in this manner. That may sound extreme to some of you, and to some of my friends they think it is, but it's what works for my family. Other people may be comfortable with more time, but I am not. Every family has their own rules around electronics, and the rules at my house are a bit different than the rules at their dad's house when it comes to their devices, but he always respects the 30-minute rule on school nights. They aren't missing out on anything, and their concentration is better, along with their attitudes and behaviors with fewer electronic interferences.

Here's the thing about electronics, they are not developmentally appropriate. They're barely developmentally appropriate for fully grown and functioning adults. Phones are addictive. Social media is addictive. In order to write this chapter and be sure to reach my word count goal of the day I'm sitting here with my phone turned upside, down just so I don't see the notifications.

The fact that I just wrote that sentence makes me want to check my phone, because someone on Facebook might be awake, and they might have updated their status, and if I don't check it right now I'm going to miss it and find myself out of the loop. How ridiculous is that?

I know I'm not the only one out there that has become attached to their phone. If I left my phone home on the way to town or work,

I'm turning around to go get it. Most of us would. We feel naked without our phones, and we are adults.

Children also become attached, but here's the thing, electronics and especially social media is extremely damaging to children's brain development. Handing your child an electronic device when they're young is equivalent to taking them to play the slots at the casino. I don't say that to be harsh. I say that because it's the truth. We are addicted to our devices because our brains fill up with dopamine every time a notification goes off. Every time someone comments on something. Every time your phone lights up, your pleasure section of your brain is activated and tells you that you need more of it. The same thing happens to children playing tablets, or handheld video games. That pleasure center is being saturated in dopamine telling them that they need more of it, right now. Right now.

Dopamine is also what is released in the brains of gamblers, and addicts of any kind. This is why addicts just can't stop. Their dopamine receptors are used to being oversaturated with dopamine, so when they're walking around with their normal level of dopamine trying to do their dopamine job, their brain is pushing the panic button. Their brain is saying wait a darn minute, my dopamine is contained to these receptors and they need to be overflowing.

When you give your two-year-old a tablet and don't regulate its use, you are allowing your toddler's dopamine to overflow, teaching their brain that it needs this overabundance of dopamine to function. This *will* come out in their behavior. It always does.

Children that are not given age appropriate restrictions on electronics do not regulate their feelings well, especially when the electronics are removed for disciplinary reasons. Children that are addicted to their devices can be irritable, angry, easily frustrated, have a short attention span, and may even have core muscle weakness. They may have trouble in school, they may be forgetful or disorganized. Addiction to devices can look and sound a lot like ADHD.

When kids get a little older, parents are more likely to allow their child to have social media accounts earlier than they should, because in a way, parents have become desensitized to the idea. Their kid has had a phone since they were four, why wouldn't they feel like by nine, their kid can have an Instagram account? If you don't believe me, just scroll through Instagram and see how many little ones have their own accounts.

Social media drives self-esteem issues. Social media is the catalyst to bullying. Placing social media in the hands of a pre-teen or early teenager, and letting them have full access, unregulated aside from the random checks you do of their messages (kids are more tech savvy than you, they delete their messages and disable features you set up) are a recipe for in school and online bullying.

In school bullying sucks, but they come home from school. Online bullying doesn't stop. They hear it in school, then come home and hear the same things or worse because there are no teachers or parents in earshot. Sometimes it doesn't even have to be bullying.

Preteens are just developing their sense of who they are in the world in relation to everyone else. They're beginning their gangly and awkward stage, and just as they're feeling weird inside of their own bodies, parents allow them to have social media.

I want you to think about the last time you saw an old high school friend on the internet living their best life. Think about when Carol had her third baby and was posting sizzling selfies at the beach three weeks later, while you're at home with your ten-year-old that you still haven't lost your muffin top from. How does that make you feel? Probably a little self-conscious. This is what is being fed to our kids when they are allowed to have phones and then social media early.

It's tough, I completely understand, but regulating the amount of time on devices is so important to a child's development. How many times have we seen a toddler acting out and instead of pulling out a toy or a book, the parent gives them their phone? Dopamine. A preschooler is misbehaving at dinner in a restaurant, mom pulls out a tablet. Dopamine. Three-year-old wailing on the floor at Target, mom pulls out a phone and turns it to YouTube. Dopamine.

We are constantly rewarding unwanted behaviors with yummy natural brain chemicals that tell them they need more of it to function. Look, I know it's hard. I know you get embarrassed. But, it's not your job to please the people of Target, or Olive Garden.

Your job is to raise a good human. Your job is to make sure your child is developing appropriately. That is your job.

Did you know, children that are introduced to tablets in early toddler years have delayed speech development? There was a study done on it recently. Toddlers, preschoolers, and school-agers have trouble with impulse control. These natural impulse control issues are exacerbated by electronics. By the school age years, children should be gaining more self-control, but video games tell them they get what they want now, so they have trouble waiting.

So, parents, if you are really wanting to get a head start on positive behaviors from your little ones, do your future self a favor and leave the electronics for the adults, or at the very least older teenagers. You will thank yourself later when your kid is building rocket ships out of old boxes and crayons. You'll thank yourself when you don't have to constantly stimulate your child with some form of entertainment because they have learned to entertain themselves with their imaginations.

Do you know that many things are invented or created because someone allowed themselves to be bored? I truly cannot stress the importance of learning how to be bored is. There are going to be times where your child is forced to wait. There are going to be times when they have to use their imagination. Don't put that light out before it even gets the flame going.

4
Let There Be Tantrums

I'm sure you're looking at the title of this chapter like "what you talkin' 'bout Willis?" But hear me out. Tantrums happen. Tantrums are always going to happen. I don't care who you are, or what you do for a profession. You could be the author of a book about parenting, and your kid will still throw a tantrum. Do you see what I did there? Yeah, my kids have all thrown tantrums. I mean, they don't throw them now, with the exception of my 13-month-old, well...let's be honest, sometimes my 11-year-old throws a mean tantrum. It's very dramatic. Eleven-year-old's still sometimes have tantrums y'all. This is my third time having a child this age, so I knew the tantrums would temporarily return due to an influx of new hormones. Yay for preteens! The good news you guys, is you get several tantrum free years before the preteen stage starts. So, why don't we dive in to why kids have tantrums, and why on earth people in public look at parents like they just sprouted two new heads.

You guys, tantrums are a normal part of development. I'm totally going to say that again because it bears repeating. Tantrums are a normal part of development. I have never met a child in my entire life that has never once had a tantrum. These things serve a very hefty purpose. They allow our little people's voices to be heard. They allow parents to know that their child is unhappy and therefore dysregulated. If you read the previous chapter you have learned some ways to help your child regulate their emotions. Use those. Once a child learns to regulate their emotions, they will have less tantrums as a result. But we are going to stay on topic.

Have you ever seen a kid in the middle of Walmart, or your local grocery store just having a massive earth shattering fit? How many times have you offered that befuddled parent a word of encouragement? How many times have you just walked right past, or even worse gave a dirty look and said something like "My kid would never act like that" or "That child needs some discipline?" How helpful do you think that latter response is to that parent who is obviously struggling? How helpful would it be to you? Not very. If anything, you or someone else, just helped make that parent feel even more like garbage because their child is having a hard time with their emotions.

So, let's think about why parents become so embarrassed around their kid's tantrum? Why is that embarrassing? Your child is in distress because they want something, and they were told no, or maybe their shoe feels funny because the crease of their sock is rubbing across their toes. The point is, children can throw a tantrum for any number of reasons, but they are only doing so because they are still trying to figure out these emotions and what to do with them. Let them throw their tantrum. Stand there proudly and smile at the passersby while you make sure your child is safe until they can get it together. Let them throw their tantrum and ignore the dirty looks and snide remarks about your parenting skills, because you got this. This is normal. This is parenthood. This is what children do. When your child gets up and is ready to start behaving like his normal human self, help them wipe their tears and tell them it's ok to be disappointed because they didn't get XYZ. Tell them that you love them. Give them a hug for trying to work through such a big emotion. Then tell them that next time their feelings are so big, its ok to ask for a quiet space. It's ok for them to tell you that they are mad at you. It's ok for them to express their feelings in a safe and respectful way. Our children are not robots. They're not perfect, and they are much newer at trying to regulate their emotions that you are.

Parents becoming embarrassed because their child is throwing a fit, is less about the parent, and more about the parent's fear of being judged. You are worried about the Karen's and Dave's of the world giving you dirty looks, or thinking mean or rude things to you, because seriously, they are not likely going to say anything to you about any of it. They are just going to walk by with their noses in the air like they are the best parents in the world, whether they have children or not. They don't know you. They don't know what you're trying to do. They don't know what your values are or how you're trying to raise your kid as a good human. They don't know anything about you. The only thing they know is this small moment in time. I mean, would you really want the approval of someone that is just passing by judging a parent that's simply doing their best while their child is learning to manage their emotions. Your kid is doing what kids do, and these people are giving you dirty looks. No ma'am! No! You will not allow anyone to make you feel bad about doing your very best to raise your child in a way that respects their basic human development. I don't care who is judging you. I don't care if it's the random people in Walmart. I don't care if it's your sister, or your mema. I don't care. If they're going to sit back and judge without trying to understand what you're doing, put your hater blockers on and keep it moving. You don't need their judgment, or even opinion on how you are raising your children.

I have mastered a mean side eye for those that like to pass quick judgment on a parent they know nothing about. I have learned to use my voice to call out people for being rude or unhelpful to parents that are likely just trying their best. I have learned to give a struggling parent a knowing smile, or a "this too shall pass" when I see them just barely holding it together themselves. When we judge, we have no idea what the other person is going through. This short glimpse of time that we get, is just a tiny piece of what is happening in their lives. We have to stop judging other parents, because we are the Karen's and Dave's too. So, check yourself the next time you go out. We have got to do better you guys, and the only way to do that is to start with us, not them.

Learning to deal with tantrums is challenging. We feel the judging eyes of others because we are judging ourselves. We are already questioning "am I a good mom" or "why is he acting like this, everyone is staring." Yeah, everyone is staring. Let them. You and your child are both learning, give both of you some grace. If your kid is throwing a fit in an unsafe place (like once, my daughter threw a fit in front of the doors leading out of Walmart in the garden center) move them. I drug her little body away from the door and told her that people can't get past, so she needed to throw her fit over here. Over her was in an aisle right next to the door. I moved her maybe ten feet. She continued her fit in a safe area, and I continued pretending to shop until she was finished. If you're on a time crunch and you've got to go and don't have time to wait for the tantrum to end, pick them up surfboard style or like a piece of luggage and carry them to the car. Be sure to tell them they can be upset and cry, but they have to do it in their car seat.

Some children are stronger willed than other children, and they may not cooperate enough for you to buckle them in their seats. If this is your child, it will still be OK. Carry them into the car and let them continue their tantrum. Call whomever you need to call to let them know you will be late and sit back and wait for it to pass. You cannot stop their fit without giving them what they want. If you're thinking about spanking, just let that idea drop. Spanking is not going to stop a tantrum, it will either make it worse, or just make your child start crying for a different reason. Spanking in this situation would only teach your kid two things. One they can't trust their emotions because they are being hit for having them, and two, my mom or dad can't regulate their emotions without hitting, so hitting is what I need to do when I'm angry.

How long your child's tantrum will last is mostly related to how you handle their tantrum. If you become anxious and red-faced, while doing whatever you can possible to get them to stop, they are going to keep going until they get what they were after in the first place. If you start yelling and being impatient, they're going to keep going because they're now scared. Your children are looking to you for cues on how to deal with their own tantrums. If you are calm and collected, using a soothing voice or not saying anything at all, that tantrum won't last long. They know they aren't making you upset. They know that you are still their safe place because you're allowing them to work through their feelings without trying to change them or stop them. They know that you can regulate your own feelings and they want to be like you.

5
Consistency is Your Bestie

What is this thing I speak of? Oh, it's just your best friend consistency. It's this crazy thing that keep behaviors in check. It's something that all parents have some concept of, but don't always stick with, because results aren't immediate. Let me tell you something friends, I love me some consistency! I love it! If I could marry consistency, I would, but what would that look like? Weird I'm guessing. Plus, my actual husband would probably have problem with it. I just want you to understand just how important it is, and how much I can't get enough of it. Especially for toddlers and preschoolers, and any age child you have. Consistency lets your kid know what's coming next without much thought. In fact, if your being consistent every time, all the time, your child will know what's next without thought at all. If they know what's coming, they're less likely to misbehave.

What areas in life should consistency be applied? In all areas. ALL. OF. THEM. I'm not yelling, I'm just caps locking for emphasis, so you know how serious I am. I'm super cereal guys. Like, super cereal. I'm also a dork, but I digress. The first place you want to use consistency is with routine, and later we will have a whole chapter on working out a routine for your child if you don't already have one. Once you have established a routine, and your kid knows what's next, you want to translate that into rules and consequences. There will also be a whole chapter on that, so you know what's age appropriate and what's not. But it's safe to say if you don't have consistent rules, then you child won't know what they are allowed to do, and what is off limits. Having wishy washy rules is confusing. If one day I draw on the wall and get time out, but the next time I do it, I don't get anything, what's the rule? Can I draw on the wall or not? Don't enforce rules half way. Enforce them all the way, all the time.

There seems to be some confusion about consistency within my friend group as well, so I felt like I needed to dedicate a whole chapter to it. I have a few friends that say they're consistent with their rules, but I've seen them with their kids on more than one occasion. They may have consistent rules, but their reactions and consequences to the infraction to the rules are not in the least bit consistent. You guys. You cannot be couch parents. You cannot be across the room parents. When your children are little, you've got to be up and down, I'm getting my exercise, I'm right on your level helping you figure this out kind of parent. Every. Time. Every time, guys. You cannot sit on the couch and call your kids name ten times while repeating, don't do that, and not get up until your thirteenth time saying not to do something.

When it comes to parenting I have a method of ONE, THREE, FIVE. No, I'm not yelling again. ONE: If your child is under three years old, you tell them the rule while removing them or taking action on the unwanted behavior the first time. Do not wait. Do not couch parent. At this age you are parenting for safety. So, you say your rule *as* you are moving or stopping them from doing the thing they aren't allowed to do. Will your back hurt? Yup. Do it anyway. THREE: When your child is preschool age, meaning ages 3-5, you give them a chance to work out the rule for themselves. It works like this.

You notice they are doing something wrong, or not even wrong, but against your house rules. You tell them the rule three times. By the time you get to the third time repeating the rule, you should be moving to aid them in following the rule. So, three chances. First chance, "Jimmy, don't play in the bathroom sink." Second chance, "Jimmy, don't play in the bathroom sink or you're going to time out." Third time, (you are up and moving now) "Jimmy, I have asked you not to play in the sink several times, let's go sit in time out until you can follow the rules." Does that make sense? I hope it does.

Last, but not least, FIVE: Count out loud to five. This part works like this. You tell them the rule. If they don't follow the rule, you give them the chance to follow the rule on their own by counting down. At this point the child knows the rule and knows the consequences, so it is their choice to follow the rule without you having to repeat yourself thirty times.

We are going to use Jimmy again. So yesterday, four-year-old Jimmy was playing in the sink. You told him the rule yesterday. You gave him the consequence yesterday. In fact, you've done this several times over the past several weeks, so you know for a fact that Jimmy knows the rule and the consequence for breaking the rule.

You still with me? Good. So, today Jimmy is playing in the bathroom sink again. With this part of the 1-3-5 method, you would say "Jimmy, stop playing in the sink." Jimmy will ignore you, and you know this because you can clearly still hear the water running and him splashing. Well, this time, you count to five loud enough for Jimmy to hear you. Once you get to about three, you want to be on your feet. When you get to five, you take little Jimmy to time-out while reminding him of the rule.

The 1-3-5 method is what I have used on all of my children and I can promise you it works. Your children learn when mom or dad says something, they mean it, and the consequences are consistent and predictable. This is what I mean by consistency, friends. Saying something 10-15 times and then waiting until you're yelling like a crazy person is not being consistent. Yes, the consequence might be the same. Might. But you have just become very dysregulated in front of your children, which is teaching them that yelling and screaming when they are frustrated is perfectly acceptable behavior.

You cannot say something more than three times without a consequence and call it consistent. You just can't. If one day you say it five times, and the next day you say it nine times, then I'm not sure of the rule. Especially if you simply give up because on this day you just can't deal with it. That's not consistency. That leaves the door wide open for unwanted behavior. Unwanted behavior leads to you being embarrassed or keeping your kids out of the public eye, simply to avoid the presumed judgement. I don't say all of this to shame you. Nothing you have done, up until right this second has been shameful. You have been doing your very best with what you had. That's nothing to be ashamed about. You are raising humans. Not just humans even, you're raising *good* humans. That takes hard work. Remember what I said before. None of us got instruction manuals when our babies were sent home. You do your best with what you have until you learn better and repeat the process.

Not knowing how to appropriately express emotion is another reason young children act out. Heck, it's why some adults act out. This is a phrase I have said often, and when I say often, I mean roughly ten thousand times a day. The phrase is "use your words." I'm sure if there were a Guinness World Record on this phrase, I would have beaten it. Why is it so hard for kids to remember to use their dang words?! You know why, we reviewed it several times already. It doesn't make it any more fun to keep repeating this phrase. This phrase, and "I can't understand you when you whine."

Oh, my goodness you guys, I just can't deal with that phrase any longer, but I thought It'd be a great idea to have another baby in my late thirties, so I guess I should prepare myself for this phrase to be figuratively tattooed across my tongue once my new toddler learns to speak more than two letter words. These phrases are part of the consistency chapter, because you have to say them all the time, every time. Example. Bobby is two, and has been trying to stack blocks, but they keep falling. Bobby gets angry and kicks the blocks and starts crying. You would say, "Use your words, Bobby. Are you mad?" It's assumed that Bobby is old enough to say simple words. Again, we are giving their emotion labels. This is important for language development, and emotional intelligence. It would also be used in a situation where Bobby is just crying and clinging to you, and you have no idea why. Reminding them to use their words allows them to know that we care and want to understand their needs.

Don't get me wrong, encouraging kids to use their words, or saying that you can't understand them when they whine are great tools to keep in your tool box. They teach children effective communication without crying or tantrums. It's just that when you're doing it like you're supposed to, it makes you want to roll your eyes so hard that they get stuck in the back of your head. Raising children that don't whine and throw fits whenever things don't go their way is hard work, and you have to commit to putting in the work if you want to do this successfully. You can't half-way your way through this process.

If I were a swearing person, you know what I would've said. You cannot half-tail your way through parenting. If you're halfway doing it, I encourage you to jump in completely and see the difference in your children's behavior. Parenting is a job, and you have to dedicate your attention to being consistent to make your life easier and provide your child with healthy boundaries.

6
Boundaries and Behaviors

Does your kid have boundaries? Yes, they do? That's great! Are their boundaries age appropriate? Yes, they are? That's awesome! Kids need boundaries. In some of the earlier chapters, I gloss over boundaries and how to enforce them. I didn't go into a lot of detail, because I knew that this glorious chapter was coming up soon. Don't fret, this won't be a long chapter, but I did think it needed to be its own chapter, so it didn't get lost with the overload of information you might be feeling. To some, boundary setting may seem like common sense, but to others this is novel information. Though, I don't think anyone is just letting their kid run around being a heathen, no matter what you may be thinking internally when you notice that one kid screaming and knocking things off the shelves. Chances are Damien over there also has some sort of boundaries. His boundaries might be a lot looser than the boundaries you'd set for your own children, but I'm almost positive he has basic ones set, like, don't touch the stove, or don't run with scissors.

Basic boundaries are great, because usually those are the safety boundaries. Safety boundaries are the boundaries we set when our children are exploring infants and cruising toddlers. We set these basic boundaries before we even realize that's exactly what we are doing. We cover light sockets, put little boxes around the television cords, and place baby gates at the top and bottom of stairs, and in entry ways. The moment our baby is trying to move, we set physical basic boundaries. The locks on the cabinet, boundary. The playpen, boundary. Baby proofed cabinets, boundary. We set boundaries on their entire lives, but for some reason, once they get a little older, some people relax their boundaries on their children. Your child can now walk and talk? Sweet, your boundaries for them change, but they don't relax.

Let's think about appropriate boundaries for toddlers and preschoolers. So, we still want to account for safety. Toddlers boundaries will still mostly be around keeping them safe, so don't take the baby gates down just yet, unless they have started scaling them to climb over. If your toddler has still not figured out how to open the gates, and cannot climb over them, keep them up. It's nice to have a space they can be in that's completely child proofed, so you can get some things done.

Now, I don't know how your home is set up, but my kitchen has a passthrough window, so I can see what my toddler is doing while I'm preparing his lunch. Another boundary you might add when your infant moves into toddlerhood is not touching certain things. Like remotes.

Television remotes come to mind because my son is obsessed with them. He has put together that they do something to the television, so he fights to press the buttons as soon as he gets his chubby little hands on it. It honestly doesn't bother me, but I don't want him to somehow un-program it, because I'm not tech savvy and would hate to call the cable guy back out here, just to program my remote control. Not hitting or biting. Toddlers can't talk, and if they are talking, its barely decipherable, and it's only a few words that make sense. Because toddlers can't talk, they tend to hit and bite out of frustration, and as a way to communicate. Obviously, these are not acceptable behaviors, so we place boundaries on them.

Before we move on from hitting and biting, let me tell you, this is normal. If I could shout this at you while shaking your shoulders, I would. Daycare centers, and sometimes, other parents act like hitting and biting means your child is likely rabid and you're doing something all wrong. These behaviors are normal. Full stop. Do not feel bad because your child has taken up hitting or bit someone at daycare. This is a developmentally normal behavior for a toddler. Normal. Nothing is wrong with your child. I felt like I needed to take a minute to tell you that because I have heard from other professionals about how someone else's child is "bad" because they bit someone.

They are not bad. Frustrated. Overwhelmed. Confused. Annoyed. Tired. Any of those things, but they are not being bad. The best way to set boundaries around hitting and biting behaviors is to immediately correct the behavior sternly and tell them it hurts. You do not bite them back. You do not hit them back. Let me say this one more time for the people in the cheap seats.

Do not bite your toddler back. Do not hit your toddler back. As frustrated as you might be, this is not an appropriate response. If you bit or hit your child, you are teaching them that when you get frustrated, it's OK to hit and bite, which is the exact opposite of what you are trying to teach them. Boundary setting is hard, especially with toddlers who barely understand what you're trying to do. They're just trying to live their best life, and for some reason the big people in the house are trying to stop them.

Continuing on the topic of hitting and biting. If you get frustrated or angry with your child because they keep hitting you or biting you, tap out. Yes, I mean tap out. You can't parent through that kind of frustration. Ask for help. If you have a partner at home or even an older child that can keep an eye on your kid for five minutes while you collect yourself, ask for help. It doesn't make you a bad parent. It makes you a better parent. Know your limits and tag someone else in. I'm not kidding on this one.

You may think it's something you can power through, but if you are seeing red, you cannot effectively parent. Remember earlier when we talked about managing big emotions? It's not just little ones that have a difficult time thinking and processing big emotions. So, what do you do if you're the only person home? You can call over a neighbor, or you can place your child in their crib, or their childproofed room, and step outside on the porch for a few minutes. Take some deep breaths, call you mom or another mom friend. Go back inside and parent from a more relaxed place. I'm not talking about going for a twenty-minute walk while your kid is inside screaming their head off, I'm talking about staying within earshot and taking five or so minutes to get yourself together, mama. Parenting is not for the faint of heart.

Boundary setting for preschoolers, will be different than toddlers. What you are doing is building off of each stage of boundaries. We don't relax the boundaries set in previous stages, we add to them, with the exception of some of the baby proofing. Obviously, you don't need to keep up baby gates when your child is four or five, chances are, they've learned how to open them anyway. With preschoolers, you are able to communicate on a more sophisticated level, and their boundaries will also be a little more sophisticated. Though, we are just building off of previously set boundaries, you can now explain why some rules are in place. This is such a nice step in boundary setting. People, children included, are more likely to follow a rule when they know why a rule is put in place. The line "because I said so" should be left in the past. It doesn't work. Simple age appropriate explanations only aid in more effective parenting. Preschoolers boundaries may look like being allowed to make their own snack with supervision, but you're still going to be working on not hitting our friends at this age. Reinforcing using our words to communicate and allowing more supervised freedoms are key to positive behaviors.

Figuring out what boundaries to set for your child in your home are mostly unique to your family. There are some that should probably be non-negotiables. Here are some non-negotiables in my home. Don't stand next to the stove while something is cooking without an adult present. Don't run out into the street. No running in parking lots. Always hold a hand or onto a piece of clothing worn by an adult or older sibling when walking in a parking lot or crossing the street. No running up and down the steps. Don't get a snack without asking. No going outside without an older sibling or an adult. As you can see, some rules are safety issues, and some are just unique to my home. I don't like when my kids get snacks, because they will eat them all. Anyone that has had children home during school breaks knows they will eat snacks like starving velociraptors. So, that's just a rule we've had since preschool. What you decide are your non-negotiable rules are going to be different than someone else's, and that's great. It works for you and your family! Just be consistent with whatever rules you set.

You may be wondering how boundaries play into behaviors. Having clear and consistently enforced boundaries help children know what is expected of them. If children know what is expected of them, they are less likely to misbehave because they know what the rules are, and you've been consistent with the consequences when rules are broken.

7
Choosy Moms Choose Choices

I try to think of catchy titles for these chapters, but this title might be kind of lame. Eh, it's fine. Throughout this book I'm giving you all of my secrets on why and how my children are so well behaved. These are all things that I learned while getting my undergrad degree in child development, and also things I realized are not taught to the majority of parents in a way that they can digest. My hope is that you are able to digest this in a way that can you learn to apply it to your life, and your children. When my children were little, choices were my children's friend. Children enjoy feeling like they have some autonomy in their lives. Most of their lives are dictated for them, so allowing them to have choices over a few things empowers them and cuts down on tantrums.

When I say allow your child to make their own choices, I'm not talking about big things. I'm talking about things that won't make a difference in the grand scheme of your life. Do you want the blue or red cup? Do you want an orange or a cheese stick? Do you want to wear jeans or joggers? These are not earth-shaking choices. When my daughter was four, she wore a Snow White costume nearly every day for a month. Sometimes she was Snow White with butterfly wings, and sometimes she was Snow White with a Dora backpack. She wore the plastic little heels that came with her original costume, and I allowed her to continue to make that choice whenever appropriate. At the time she was in a Catholic preschool, so she had to wear a uniform most days, until school was out, but once school was over, the costume went on instead of whatever street clothes she had. I could have fought her on it, and made her wear something that resembled normal clothing, but it wasn't important. She was happy, and comfortable. She was appropriately covered, and not hurting anyone.

This was her thing, and I wasn't going to take it away from her. I certainly wasn't going to discourage her from expressing herself. And you know what, this built her confidence. She has continued to wear whatever she wants without the care of anyone else's judgement. There was a day during her junior year of high school that she actually wore a tail, you guys. A. Tail. My child, got dressed in a black skirt, knee socks with cats on them, put on some cat ears, and pinned a tail to her waistband. She wore that thing to school without a second thought.

I think about how when I was 16, I wouldn't have dared to step outside the norm, but my daughter did it whenever the mood struck her. Seeing her do this reaffirmed that allowing her to make her own choices in childhood was confidence boosting. She was able to navigate high school unscathed, and unbothered by the mean girls. She's still a confident person when it comes to her decisions. She knows what she wants, and she goes after it. She's not afraid to tell people no for fear of hurting their feelings. My daughter is a freaking Rockstar!

Choices are confidence boosting, and they save on drama. How many times do you struggle to get your kid out of the house because they want to wear clothes that don't match? Or they throw a tantrum because they wanted cereal, but you gave them oatmeal. If it's a simple meal, you don't have to fight with your child. You can let them make the small choices and save yourself some grief. We can let them have some control over their own lives.

If we don't allow them to make choices now, in the comfort of our homes, then how are we going to expect them to make the harder choices later. We have got to allow them the room to choose. If we don't allow our children any choices they feel smothered with rules, and if you've ever been smothered with rules, be it at home, or at work, then you are familiar with what comes next. Rebellion. Your child is going to begin to buck the system. It's just that simple.

A few years ago, I was asked to aid a struggling mom figure out a way to get a handle on her children's behaviors. This mom homeschooled her children, and her children were fairly well behaved in public spaces, but when they got home all heck broke loose. We sat down at the local library and went through their daily routine. I noticed a trend.

This mom did everything for her children, and they were on such a tight schedule, there wasn't room to breathe out of sync with the rest of the family. I'm not exaggerating, there isn't much room to exaggerate. Everything was planned, and the punishments were harsh. Her children were older school-agers. So, between the ages of 9-11. Their mother even picked out their clothes for the day. Their clothes! The first thing I pointed out was their lack of choices. She was shocked, guys! It hadn't occurred to her to allow her kids to make choices. It didn't dawn on her that this could be an issue. She was a great mama, and I definitely made sure to give her that praise, but she thought that in order to have well behaved children, that she needed to have control over all aspects of their lives.

Ultimate control does not create well behaved children, it creates sneaky children who don't tell you what they're up to. It creates children who don't know how to make healthy social and personal decisions, because they've never been afforded the ability to do so. It can be tempting to make every choice imaginable for your child as a way to protect them from themselves and the world. After all, you're the adult. You know what's best for them, so why let the consequences from their decisions hurt their feelings, when you can just avoid it all together by doing it for them. Sister, I feel you.

Boundaries are life. Boundaries are structure, and children need and crave structure, so I can understand where the confusion my come in. Children thrive in a structured environment, but structure does not need to be stifling. I'm sure you have heard the saying about holding a bird in your hand too tightly. We still need to allow children the room to be who they are meant to be.

Their personalities are there for a reason and should be respected. Balancing between structure and overbearing decision making for your children can be a difficult thing for some parents. But when balancing anything, you have to take a little from each side to make sure the scale is in harmony.

Not allowing for decisions, and subsequently failures when poor decisions are made will come back to bite you in the butt. I know, that is such a crude expression, but I couldn't think of a better term to use to express my point. Children that don't know how to make decisions turn into teenagers that don't know how to make decisions, which turns into adults that can't make decisions. When teens can't make decisions, who do you think makes their decisions for them when you aren't around? Their friends. Or at least who you hope they are your child's friends.

It's just when drugs or alcohol come up, and you have not allowed room for them to make their own decisions, it doesn't matter what you taught them to say because they don't have practice, and their friends are powerful forces at that age and stage. You are their safety net. You are there for them when they make the wrong choices, but you are also there to help them celebrate when they make the right decisions. Use that and open up the door for your child to become a fully functioning capable adult. Sometimes we parents forget that we are not raising children.

No one grows up from childhood to be a child. We grow up to be adults. The kind of adult we will raise is determined now, while they are still children and can be easily molded. Even if it doesn't feel so easy right now, just remember that it is easier to address and correct negative behaviors as a child, than it ever will be to fix a broken adult.

Helping your child make positive choices could be a whole chapter in itself, especially for older children, but since we are focusing on the littles here, I'll keep it brief and age appropriate. Helping a toddler or preschooler make good choices is fairly simple. It happens most often with redirection and some gentle guidance. Toddlers typically don't play well with others, because everything is theirs. Even when it's not, it's theirs. During times like these we can work on learning to share, not hitting, and not biting. These are all good choices. I know, you're probably thinking "duh," but these are the moments that they learn.

Preschoolers can still struggle with sharing and redirecting to a positive behavior with this age group is also appropriate. Preschool is also a good age to instill helpfulness. Kids this age love to feel like they are helping or in charge of something. It teaches them responsibility, as well as choosing helpfulness when others may not.

Challenging preschoolers to use their voice to stand up for their friends is a lifelong lesson that will follow them to adulthood. Let's teach our children to make good choices now, so we don't have to later.

8

Shake Your Groove Thing & Eat a Carrot

Me and these titles, man! I'm just having too much fun, and if no one else gets them or thinks they're funny, it's OK because my kids and I had a good chuckle. In this section of the book we are going to talk about some things that parents may not consciously consider when they think about altering a child's unwanted behaviors. Releasing excess energy is something that not only helps lower the stress level of the parent, but also aids in keeping your child focused long enough to hear your full instructions. You may be thinking, they are hearing everything you're saying, but I can guarantee their attentions span is about the length of a gnat's.

Part of this is due to them being easily distractible to anything shiny, or loud, or blue, or quiet, or basically anything at all that is not coming out of your mouth. The other part is because they've got all of this extra energy that they are not using, and I don't know if you've ever been around kids, which I assume you have because you're reading this book and you likely have one or three, but they need to move. Like, absolutely need to move. Sitting your kid in front of the TV or an iPad is not allowing for them to release that overabundance of stored energy.

This is definitely an area where you can be creative. Moving can come in so many forms. I have one friend that takes her early elementary schooler running with her. Her daughter has been running with her since she was three years old. This little baby had her own official running shoes and everything! It was probably the most adorable thing that I've ever seen. Y'all, this little girl was running miles by the time she was five. WHOLE MILES!!! I used to wait for this friend to upload pictures of their post run sweaty selfie. It was absolutely the best motivator to get other parents encouraged enough to move their, and their children's bodies. I watched as two other friends dipped their toe into the running journey with their children. For me, running is my selfcare, and there are no children allowed during mama's selfcare time. Selfcare is for another chapter, though, so stay tuned. You didn't think this book was going to be completely about your kid, did you? Parents need some love too, so stick around and you'll get one full chapter dedicated to you. Girl Scouts honor. Is that a thing? I don't know, I was never a Girl Scout. It just sounded like the right thing to say.

When my kiddos were toddlers and preschoolers, we danced. We danced it out every single chance we got, and they loved it. Laurie Berkner Band was definitely our jam. If you've never had the pleasure of listening to her music, I'd suggest starting with the song about her having a cow on her head. It's hilarious, has a good bounce to it, and your kids will think it is rib tickling good fun. When we weren't listening to her, we were listening to Kids Bop or whatever the Top 40 was. We would blast that music and dance as hard as we could, incorporating swing, and jazz dance moves, that none of us could do properly, but we tried. We held hands and ran around singing the words to the song as loudly as our lungs would let us. When I say we danced, we danced. We danced like nobody's business, and we did it until we were out of breath and our muscles were threatening to give out.

The best part about it was, when we were done, they were tired and had the ability to listen to the things that I was saying. I didn't have to compete with the noise in their heads or the bouncy balls in their knees. They expended their excess energy and were ready to listen. Were our dance parties planned? No. Most of the time I put music on before I needed their undivided attention, or before I needed them to sit for a longer than normal period of time; usually when I made dinner or wanted to complete a project with them.

The point of all of this is to say that movement not only helps their little brains develop, helps with coordination and large motor skills, it also helps with attention span, and the sitting still sillies. Even as adults we have a hard time sitting still when we are full of energy. Have you ever tried to sit through a meeting after drinking more than one cup of coffee? Everything is a distraction. Did my phone buzz? No? Well, did I turn my phone on silent? Yup. Why did Gina wear that awful yellow sweater? We have all done it. Our attention goes to something else, anything else that's in the room other than the person running the meeting. Our leg starts bouncing. We get up for water or go to the bathroom for the third time in an hour. If you go to the bathroom one more time, people are going to thing you're either on drugs, or have a bladder problem. Either way, you know you should force yourself to sit down and pay attention. Imagine what it's like when you're a kid. If we adults can barely keep it together when we have too much energy, how can we expect little ones who are just barely learning how to control their bodies to keep it together long enough to listen to multi-step directions? We shouldn't.

Food also plays a part in behavior. Maybe not in the way you're thinking, but I think most parents know that filling your kid with Skittles and Kool-Aid before bed is a bad idea. Children should have a fairly balanced diet, but hey, we do the best we can, right? Trying to incorporate healthy snacks and meals more often than not could have a positive effect on your child's behavior. I read several years ago about a study that focused on the outcome of removing red and yellow dyes from a child's diet to decrease ADHD symptoms. I'm not sure if that actually works, but you can look up the article and give it a try. After I read the article explaining this possible miracle cure for children diagnosed with ADHD, I started looking for the dyes in foods just to see. It was in just about everything that was processed. If you don't know what processed food is, which, I must admit, I did not understand the difference even when I had my second child...anyway, if you don't know what it is, processed foods are basically any foods that come in some sort of preserving package. So, things like cereal, American cheese, Pop Tarts, frozen pizza, lunch meat. Basically, anything that is designed to make cooking a little easier for you. I know, bummer! To be honest with you, this is part of the reason I didn't attempt to eliminate the dyes from my kids' foods. I'm so busy, and I've always been busy, I just needed the convenience of processed food.

    I did my best to pick out the healthiest options for my family, and you should too. Though, having all organic and unprocessed foods would be ideal, I understand we don't live on the Little House on the Prairie. And to be honest, who would want to? Not I, said the cat. Not I. As parents we do the best we can, and I will continue to reinforce that. It would be easy for me to sit here and lie to you. You don't know me. I could tell you that my kids eat all organic all the time. I could say that I make them kale and pineapple smoothies for breakfast and pack their lunches with handpicked fresh blueberries from our backyard. But, I'm not a liar. I'm not raising liars, and I'm not in the habit of being a liar.

    My kids do not eat all organic. The blueberries in their lunch are handpicked by someone in Chile. I know this because that's what the sticker says on the package that I bought from Walmart. If you want the full truth, I didn't even handpick the handpicked package. I use Walmart Pick-Up. I use Walmart Pick-up because I absolutely hate nothing more in this world than grocery shopping. I hate the crowds. I hate the aisles. I hate the sound the registers make as they scan your stuff. I just hate everything about it. So, yeah, I don't personally go grocery shopping for my children, and I don't feed them unprocessed foods, but you should feed it to your kids if you can, if you can't, they will survive.

The reason I'm even mentioning eating habits, is because it might help someone that is struggling with behaviors that could very well be related to poor eating habits. Getting a balanced meal in your kid's belly is important. Figuring out creative ways to get veggies down their throats is a priority, and you should absolutely strive for getting as many healthy things in your kid as possible throughout the day. Just understand that if that's not your thing, then it may be harder to get creative with it, but it doesn't mean you shouldn't try. So, if you're trying to give your little one healthy snacks and meals, pat yourself on the back. You're doing an awesome job, and I truly mean that! Do your best to cut back on the sugar and add the healthy stuff when and where you can.

One way that I cut back on the sugar is adding water to the little's juice. I do half water, and half juice. An easy healthy breakfast that may be a little processed, but it's what I have time for, and I don't feel guilty for feeding it to my kids, is Cheerios with strawberries or bananas. I will usually broil a piece of cheese toast to go on the side. For lunch or dinner, a meal typically looks like a protein, such as chicken or beef or some sort, a veggie or two, and a starch/carb. Nothing too fancy, but something easy, practical and fairly balanced. How can you beat yourself up when you're feeding them something they will eat, and something that is in the realm of healthy? You can't, so if you're doing that you have my permission to stop. When my daughter was around two years old, there was a several months stretch where she refused to eat anything but macaroni and cheese. We tried everything to get her to eat her food but trying to negotiate healthy eating with a two-year-old is like negotiating with a terrorist. She would seal her mouth shut so tightly, nothing was getting past her lips, so there were several nights she went to bed hungry because I was taught that "you eat what I make you or you starve" was the right way to go, and if I gave into refusals, then I was doing it wrong.

I quickly began to realize the flaw in this thinking. I partly came to this realization because we happened to be covering the toddler years in one of my undergrad classes at this time, and partly because it just wasn't working and felt wrong. Not feeding my child, when I knew she was hungry all because she wouldn't eat what I made her went against every instinct in my mommy body, so I stopped fighting those instincts, no matter what my mother or grandmother said. I knew my kid liked mac and cheese, so I gave her mac and cheese. I gave her mac and cheese with peas in it. I snuck in corn, and green beans, and occasionally I could sneak in some ground beef or ground turkey.

You know what happened when I started feeding her what I knew she would eat? Well, she ate. She ate some version of macaroni and cheese every single day until she felt like she had some sort of control over things in her itty-bitty life. Eating is one of the first things children realize they can control. It's also one of the things that drive a parent crazy when their child is refusing it. Her pediatrician once told me, "she will eat when she's hungry." This was well meaning advice, and works with most kids, but my daughter, who we would later found out was on the higher end of the spectrum, had issues with the texture of food playing into her refusal to eat. Once I relinquished a little bit of control, I found more foods that she would eat, that didn't feel weird on her tongue.

I know you've heard the term, every child is different. That is absolutely correct. I have four children and each one of them, though raised the same way, are completely different from each other. My boys have never had issues with eating what I put in front of them. They didn't care if it was pizza or a veggie tray, they ate it with the same excitement that they would eat gummy bears. My daughter on the other hand was a completely different beast when it came to food.

Through her, I learned you can only do what you can do. Your child is a whole human person with their own likes and dislikes. So, if you're having issues getting your kid to eat something healthy, get creative. There is more than one way to skin a cat. I'm not advocating skinning cats, I live in the south, so we say strange colloquialisms like these. No cats were harmed in the writing of this book.

9

The Fabulous RRC's

What are The RRC's? Settle in and give this chapter a thorough read. The RRC's are a game changer for parenting successfully. Chances are you are using some version of this whether you realize it or not. And you may not be. I don't know, so that's why I'm including it in this book. This is also something I learned in school, I know, it's crazy. Who would've thought I'd learn something valuable after spending $38K to get a piece of paper with my name on it?! Lucky for my oldest, she got to be my guinea pig as I learned these new concepts when she was a toddler and preschooler. She's a functioning adult, so was no long-term damage done.

This is also something that I teach friends and clients that come to me wanting to know how to consistently manage their child's behaviors. I go over it with them in detail and offer to help them create a chart, which will be included in this book, so you can see what it looks like. You can create the chart on the computer, which is what I do, because I'm not a crafty mom, and I can't draw a straight line with a ruler. A chart requires several straight lines. I'm going off into a tangent. SO, what exactly *are* The RRC's? Rules, Rewards, and Consequences. I know you're thinking that doesn't seem like it's some sort of holy grail. I told you guys you likely already use them, so don't give me that look, but do hear me out.

Most households with children have some sort of version of this going on. Unless you're raising free range children with no boundaries, you have rules. You probably have consequences. A lot of families even have the rewards system in place. So, this is not a unique concept. The thing that is unique, is that you write this down in a chart for everyone to see. Yes, even the littles that can't read yet. There is something wonderful that happens when this is laid out in chart form. There is no confusion.

The issue I find most when working with families, is that the big people in the house aren't on the same page. I'm looking at you moms, dads, and grandparents. Aunts and uncles, you don't get to escape this either. If the adults that help raise the children aren't on the same page then it doesn't matter what one parent does, or how consistent they are, the children are not going to behave in a way that you find acceptable because the rules are different depending on who's home. This just doesn't work. I think everyone can think of a situation that they've been in, either growing up, or in the workforce, where the rules were inconsistent depending on who was present. One supervisor was a stickler for rules and policy, while the other supervisor was like "I don't care if you cut out this step," and you just try to adapt to whoever was supervising you at the moment. It's confusing. You just want to know the rule that is actually the rule and not supervisor preference, so you can do your job effectively. So, I'm going to take a moment to break down The RRC's for you, and at the end of this chapter, I'll have them laid out in a handy sample chart.

Rules: These should be reasonable and consistent across the board no matter where you are, or who they are with. So, this means, just because you guys are at grandma's house doesn't mean there are different rules. When you go to the library or Target, the rules are the same. Obviously for each section of the RRC's, you need to make sure there is age appropriateness. You wouldn't have the same rules for a two-year-old as you would have for a five-year-old, but no matter what they need to be consistent. For example, the other day I was visiting my friend, and my one year old started trying to open all of her kitchen cabinets. The rule in our house is that he can't open the kitchen cabinets. We have a gate to keep him out of the kitchen, but he can come in when there is an adult in the kitchen as well. Yes, we lock the cabinets with cleaning supplies in it. Well, at my friend's house he keeps trying to open the cabinets, and I tell him no and remove him, and he would stop for a few minutes then try again. This is just the process of enforcing a rule with littles. My friend says, "oh he can play in this cabinet." What a sweet, well-meaning thing to say. I said OK, and continued to move him and tell him no. Not because I wanted to ignore that she said it was fine for him to do, but because that is my rule at my house. The purpose is that he doesn't get into something at someone's house that he's not allowed to have. People keep all kinds of things in their cabinets, and I'd like for him not to explore them, so I redirected him to things he is allowed to play with. He didn't care and stopped trying after about five minutes. He knows the rule, even at 13 months old. He knows the rule because it's always the same no matter who is in the kitchen with him.

Rewards: This is an area that some experts disagree on. Some people feel that you shouldn't reward positive behavior, because children should do things out of the intrinsic nature of their hearts. I've worked with children for well over a decade, and I can't give you an example of one child that did not benefit behaviorally from being rewarded. I'm not saying it has to be an elaborate reward, it can be something small. Something as insignificant and a fuzzy puff ball that people use for crafts. Do you know what kind of chores little ones would do for a little puff ball to go in a jar? I say a jar, because it can be part of your system. Toddlers and preschoolers need something tangible they can see and touch. You can't tell them I'm going to put a point in my book. No, they need a sticker, a marble, a puff ball, something they can feel. The system is set up to where at the end of the week, if they have X amount of balls they can pick something out of the treasure box. When my kids were this age, the treasure box was one of those Glad Take and Toss containers, and it was filled with toys and stickers from the Dollar Tree. If I wanted to put something really fancy in there, I'd go to the $5 and under section at Target. Each rule on the chart was rewarded with a shiny rock (that I also picked up from the Dollar Tree). When they reached at least 10 rocks for the week, they got to pick from the treasure box. That's not to say that there are some things that shouldn't be done for their intrinsic value. Absolutely, there are things that even as a preschooler should be done out of the goodness of their hearts. For my family it was telling the truth. On their RRC chart, telling the truth reaped the reward of the warm and fuzzy feeling of knowing you're an honest person. My chart legitimately said that. There was most definitely a consequence for lying, so just because there isn't a tangible reward for certain things on the chart doesn't mean there shouldn't be a consequence if the rule is broken. I'd suggest giving these types of rules a light sprinkling on your chart. We only had one rule that didn't have a tangible reward attached to it.

Consequences: OK, I'm going to be a little stern right here, because some people do not understand how to administer appropriate consequences. Your consequences absolutely should not only be age appropriate, but developmentally appropriate. There is no reason for a three-year-old to be in time out for thirty minutes. None. The time out rule is always one minute per year of age. This means, if your child is three, they should only be in time out for three minutes. There is a reason for this. Toddlers have a very short attention span, and so do preschoolers, but for a toddler, you can cut that attention span in half. If you put a three-year-old in time out for longer than three minutes, they forgot why you put them there. No joke, they forgot. Once they forget your consequence is no longer effective, and is no longer even a consequence, it's a punishment. And to them, you're just being mean, because they have no idea why they are being made to stay in time out, because they no longer remember what landed them there. Same goes for long consequences for preschoolers. You cannot take a toy away from a four or five-year-old for a week and think they will have learned their lesson. They didn't. They forgot why you removed the toy in the first place. In many cases, they forgot they even had the toy to begin with. I know you may be thinking that I'm over exaggerating, but I'm really not. Most children that young cannot remember what they did to deserve the consequence to begin with if the consequence is abnormally long. The idea of out of proportion punishments also go for physical punishments, and I call them punishments because if a parent is doing something physical to their child as a means to correct behavior, they are punishing them, not giving them a consequence. There is nearly no natural consequence that would result in a physical result. I'm not only talking about spanking. Like I mentioned earlier, I live in the south, experts can pry spanking out of the cold dead hands of most southerners. I'm talking about really harsh and psychologically damaging physical punishments. I've seen some parents, and even teachers making children as young as five do wall sits or motorcycle stands until tears were rolling and the kids were begging to stop. If you don't know what those are, I encourage you to look them up and then try to do them for five or ten minutes. The only thing severe physical punishments are good for, are teaching your children to be afraid of you. And if your child is afraid of you, they sure as heck aren't going to tell you when something is upsetting them or ask for advice on a situation you may not approve of later in their teens.

Natural and Logical Consequences: I debated on if I was going to include this section in the RRC's portion or give it its own chapter. When it came down to it, this is solid information, but I didn't feel like it was enough info for a whole chapter. Maybe you've heard of natural and logical consequences, or maybe you haven't. Either way, I can guarantee you everyone that is on this earth has experienced natural and logical consequences. Not you? Lies!!! Everyone has. Natural and logical consequences are things that happen without interference from another party. Have you ever heard a story and thought or said "I hope they learned their lesson." Chances are, you were talking about natural and logical consequences that person experienced. There are plenty of times when a child can learn their lesson through this process, without parent intervention. The problem is, most parents save their kid from experiences these negative consequences, therefore stifling their natural growth from experiencing these very logical results directly related to their action or inaction.

Maybe you've seen this, or maybe you have done this, but either way, we are doing our children a disservice by intervening with their natural and logical consequences. Parents are so concerned about their child being left out, or having their feelings hurt, that they rescue them at every turn. We have to stop doing that. I'm talking to you, super moms! Jonathan forgot his homework, even though you reminded him to put it in his binder before he went to bed? Oh, well. Lincoln left her lunchbox sitting on the counter? Guess she's just going to have to eat school lunch. She'll survive. Oh, Jaxon forgot to mention a school project they've known about for 6 weeks, and it's due tomorrow? Guess, you'll lose those five points a day until it gets turned in, but what I'm not going to do is run out and buy art supplies at 9:30 PM. Sorry for you, kid. Listen Linda, I'm not telling you to do anything that I wouldn't do and haven't already done.

Once when my daughter was younger, maybe 5 or 6. She was in kindergarten. Well, she was playing outside on the swing set, and when she came inside, she left her shoes outside. I told her to get her shoes. She didn't. I told her a little later, to get her shoes. She didn't but said she did. Then next morning they were still out in the yard. Did I go pick them up? Absolutely not. I told her to pick them up. I even told her they would get gross, and she made the choice not to pick them up. She went outside several more times that week, and never brought her shoes in. P.E. day rolled around. Guess who couldn't find her shoes. I said, "I thought you brought them inside?" and she admitted she hadn't. So, she runs outside at 7 AM to grab her tennis shoes. She runs inside crying approximately ten seconds later. She had slugs in her shoes.

She was devastated, and probably slightly traumatized by seeing slugs in her shoes. I didn't have to yell, I didn't have to lecture her. I told her to do something and told her the consequence of not doing it. I allowed her to make the choice to follow instructions or not. I did not rescue her. I knew what would happen. I let it happen anyway. I told her sweetly that she would just have to miss P.E. and wear her jelly shoes, or the pair of shoes she didn't like in order to participate in class. She chose to wear the tennis shoes she didn't like, and all was well. Were her feelings hurt? Yes. Did I hurt her feelings? No. I allowed her to make her own choice and experience the consequences of that choice. Did she ever leave her shoes outside again? Nope.

When my friends would see my daughter hurriedly pick up her shoes as soon as she was told, while their children still left their shoes outside for their parents to pick up, and they couldn't understand how I got her to do it without repeated instructions, or some sort of punishment. I didn't have to tell her more than once. She experienced the consequences on her own, and I didn't have to do anything. I've parented all of my children the same way. My daughter's story about the slugs is just my favorite because you really can't make up that kind of natural consequence. I don't rescue my kids. I don't believe in it, because it only teaches them to become dependent on me rescuing them in the future. My son failed 5th grade, and I let him. I spent the entire year reminding him of homework. Trying to get him to study things other than his spelling words. He didn't want to. I told him he was in danger of failing.

We met with his teachers, and they told him he was in danger of failing. They gave him every opportunity in school to make up his work and earn extra credit. Did he do it? Nope. They sent home the letter saying he was in danger of failing and we had to have another meeting with the principal and his teachers. The principal gave me the option of moving him up to the 6th grade, even though he didn't earn it. I told her to keep him where he was because that was what his grades reflected. I explained everything we tried at home, and everything his teachers tried, but he wanted to daydream or pretend to do the work while not actually doing anything. When I tell you shock rolled across this principal's face, and two of the three teachers faces, I am telling you the truth. They said I was the first parent that didn't come in yelling and crying, demanding my child be passed to the next grade when they didn't earn it. Guys, he was 9 years old. 9. Him failing 5th grade was not going to kill him. He had a July birthday anyway and was always the youngest person in class. This kid was smart enough to do the work, no learning disability, no other diagnosis that would hinder him from completing his work like everyone else. He had a case of the "I don't want to's" and that it. So, I let him fail.

 He went back to the fifth grade while all of his friends moved on to 6th. He did well the first
half of the school year, but towards the second half he started goofing off again with his work. We had one conversation, and his teacher (he had the same one from the previous year) told him he would fail again if he didn't apply himself. He finished the year with B's in nearly every subject. When he got to 6th grade we no longer had to have that conversation. In 7th grade, he checks his grades on Powerschool and inquires about things that are missing on his own. So, while allowing him to make the choice to fail 5th grade seemed harsh, and let me tell you y'all, it hurt my feelings so bad, he has figured out what he needs to do to keep that from happening again. I cried big giant real-life tears when he failed the 5th grade, but to hear his teachers in 6th grade say, "I can tell he really loves his family,

and comes from a happy home. He's one of the most confident and well-adjusted kids we have" made my heart sing with joy. We may not always like the natural and logical consequences our children experience, but we have to let them experience them anyway. It's their lesson to learn, not ours, and if we allow them to learn those lessons, the lessons will stick.

Appendix A

Rules	Reward	Consequences
Use your walking feet inside	One marble in behavior jar	You must go back and walk again
Use your inside voice	One marble in behavior jar	No marble in behavior jar
Be respectful (no talking back)	One marble in behavior jar	No TV time
Clean your room	Two marbles in behavior jar	Mom won't help you clean it later.

10

Let's Do This Again Tomorrow

We had so much fun doing that thing yesterday, let's do it again! Routines are the best thing ever invented for babies, toddlers, children, teens, and adults. So, yeah, pretty much everyone craves the structure of a routine. This is something that I've seen young parents struggle with. They might have a loose routine, but they don't have a solid one that kids know what's coming next that day, and every day after that. The biggest complaint I have heard from parents around routines, are that they interfere with what they want to do during the day. Yeah, I know. Kids are inconvenient, but for some reason we had the strong desire to continue to repopulate this big green and blue ball that we're hanging out on. Or maybe you didn't want to repopulate, and your kid was a surprise. Well, surprise chick! Kids are inconvenient. Sorry to be the bearer of that bad news. If you have a kid not on a schedule, then you likely have a grumpy child. You may not be connecting that the reason they are so moody is due to their lack of proper scheduling, but having a routine, which includes getting enough sleep will cut down on whatever level of grumpiness your little one has.

Routines don't have to be rigid, there is some room for wiggle, but bedtime is not one of them. I cannot stress the importance of sleep enough. There is no reason a 2-year-old should be going to bed at 10 PM or later and waking up at 6 AM. None. The only exception would be a parent needing to pick that child up from a sitter or something, but even then, they should be going down at a more reasonable hour. Toddlers need a minimum of 10 hours of sleep. That's minimum, but they can sleep for 10-14 hours a night, and should be taking two naps a day until they get a little older. Once they are around 2, they should take one nap a day. When kids are preschoolers they should still be sleeping 10-13 hours a night, with one nap during the day. I know not all children nap, but the routine of at least having an hour of rest time should be incorporated.

Kids need their sleep to function properly. How irritated are you when you don't get enough sleep? I know how irritated I get, and it's not pretty. It takes all of my energy just to function like a normal person when I'm sleep deprived. Imagine that, but not having the ability to properly express your feelings or regulate your emotions. That's what we are doing to our kids when we don't allow them to get enough sleep. I know it puts a damper in your plans. I know it's annoying when your kid gets cranky at 6:30 PM while you're just trying to get groceries, but your child is tired because their bedtime is at 7 PM. I completely understand how inconvenient bedtime can be when it comes in the early evening, but unless your normal day doesn't start until 11 AM, getting them to bed early evening is the healthiest option. Did I stress the importance of sleep enough? I hope I did. It's so important you guys. This is where their brains rest, and development happens. This is where they recharge into the snuggle bug you love. This is where they grow in most aspects. They need their sleep.

So, how do you start a routine? Always start with sleep. Yeah, it's still important, one sentence later. Start with sleep. What time do they wake up every morning without fail? This is their natural alarm clock, yours as well since they can't go cook themselves breakfast. Do they normally wake up at 6 in the morning? Yes? Then their bedtime should be no later than 8 PM. Yup. No later than eight o'clock guys. That is for them to get their minimum of 10 hours of sleep. If you notice they aren't getting 10 full hours, then you need to move that bedtime back another hour. So that's the first step. Start with bedtime and work backward. Now that we've figured out what time they should go to bed based on what time they wake up, we want to look at our morning routine. Everyone's morning routine will be different. Some people have additional children that need to get off to school, while some people just have the one child, or maybe you've got to get out of the house and drop the little one off at daycare or grandma's. Everyone's morning routine will be different, but they should all have some of the same elements.

What should be the staples in your morning routine? Most of you know these, but I'll list them out for people that don't. Your morning routine should consist of waking up (I know, profound stuff), brushing their teeth, them eating breakfast. Everything after that is all you. Do you boo boo, as the cool kids say. Do you. Mid-morning snack, then lunch about an hour or two after snack. Mid afternoon snack about an hour or two before dinner. Then dinner, bath, and bed. Here's a sample of my son's schedule as a 1 year old.

Jacob's Schedule

5:30-6 AM Wake up

6 AM Breakfast

6:30-9 AM Play time

9 AM Morning Snack

9:15 -11 am Play time

11 am Lunch

11:30-2 PM Nap time

2 PM Afternoon Snack

2 pm-4 pm play time

4 pm-5 pm afternoon nap

5 pm dinner

5:30-6;30 pm Daddy snuggles/play time

6:30 pm bath time

7 pm bedtime

This is my son's schedule, every day with very little variation, even on the days he goes to daycare. The only thing that really changes on daycare days are that we leave the house at 7 AM and he comes with me to drop the older boys off at school before I drop him off at daycare. His schedule in daycare is the same as it is at home. And you know what? His teachers appreciate it. They love that after a weekend at home, he doesn't come in all groggy and grumpy, because we do the same routine at home as they do in daycare. Routines are definitely a necessity to ensure you're doing everything you can to create an environment that nourishes and encourages healthy, positive behavior. I want you to take a moment and evaluate your child's schedule. Do they have a schedule? Does their schedule change depending on the day, or your mood? Look at your child's schedule. Write it down. Ask yourself where the schedule could be tightened up. Is bedtime a fly by the seat of your pants hour of the night? Are you giving them lunch whenever you feel like it, or when they tell you they're hungry? Where can you tighten up that schedule? Got it? Yay! Now, tighten it up. We can do this guys!

Now that you've gotten your child's schedule locked down, you may be wondering how on earth you are going to stick to the meal times if you're not home. No? Well go you! This part is for the parents that are wondering then. You can go grab a cup of coffee while I catch them up. So, how do we stick to a schedule when we have to be out of the house for an extended period of time? All of my children had these little backpacks. They're so cute, they're fairly cheap, and easily found at a major box store. I found my son's at Walmart for $5. Anyway, you pack their snacks, and lunch in their backpack and feed them wherever you are. I've feed my son at the doctor's office, in car rider lane, and even at soccer practice. He sticks to his schedule wherever we are. Yes, even that time we vacationed at a beach house. Inconvenient at times? You betcha, but we did it anyway.

I know there are going to be some parents who feel like their child can't be on a schedule, either because of their child's behaviors when they try to enforce a schedule, or because of their own work schedule. I know not everyone works a 9-5, and it may make more sense to you if your kid's schedule more closely resembled your own. While they are babies, and toddlers, having them on a more altered schedule may work for you, as long as they are still getting the same number of hours of sleep a child needs at their age. I would just caution you to think about preschool and elementary school. As far as I know, there is no second shift elementary school, and if their schedule doesn't shift to a more traditional one, then they may have behavioral problems in school due to a new schedule change. Changing their schedule after five years of going to bed later and waking up later will result in some unwanted consequences for both the parent and child.

11
Monkey See, Monkey Do

I know, I know, we have gone over this already. I placed it in an earlier chapter, but I only glossed over it. I didn't go into the detail I would have liked, so I'm writing this chapter at my local Starbucks before jumping into car rider lane to pick up my big boys from school. I felt like this subject deserved its own chapter. You're welcome! I truly don't believe parents give this subject enough thought or energy. They feel as though, they're teaching their children the right things, so whatever they do as parents shouldn't matter. Do as I say, not as I do. It's deja vu, I tell ya! Children very rarely do as they are told if no one is modeling the same behavior. When I was little, my mom and dad used to smoke, and would tell me not to smoke while they themselves were puffing on a cigarette. I don't smoke, but three out of four of my siblings smoke. That's not a coincidence. There are things my siblings and I buy from the store, like certain ketchup, or spaghetti sauce that we buy for no other reason than we saw our mom buying it when we were little. I'm almost 40 years old, guys, and I still copy what my parents did when I was growing up. We look to our parents for guidance on how we should act, and how we should treat other people, including our own children.

Have you ever seen a child in a classroom behaving like they had no home training, and then you meet their parents, and suddenly everything makes sense? Yeah, that's what I'm talking about. We don't come out of the womb with a road map on who to behave, so we look to our parents to show us. If our parents are showing us behavior patterns that are unacceptable, we are going to display behavior patterns that are unacceptable. Let's look at this scenario. Your child isn't doing what they're supposed to be doing, so you yell. Later in the day, their toys aren't cooperating, so they yell at their toys. You yell at them for yelling at their toys. What did that process just teach them? It taught them it's OK to yell if you're the parent. It's OK to yell if you're trying to get someone else to do what you want them to do. Is that what you meant to teach them? No, I'm sure it's not, because parents, more than anything, want to raise healthy, happy, and respectful kids. We behave in a way that is inappropriate for children to see because we are adults, and we aren't perfect, but we are in control of our own actions and we should certainly aim to display the behaviors that we would hope to see in our children.

If you want your child to be polite, then you should be polite to your child. If you want your child to be respectful, be respectful towards your child. If you want your child to use their manners, use your manners with your child. It's not some complex puzzle to figure out. If you hurt your toddler's feelings, apologize. You are not above apologizing to a two-year-old. That two-year-old has feelings, and just because they are having their behavior corrected, doesn't mean we can't apologize for hurting their feelings in the process of correcting behavior. This may seem silly to some, but I promise it's not silly. Children are still full people. Just because they are living rent free in your home, does not mean they don't deserve the same respect as a fully grown adult. Try it next time you have to discipline. It might even make you feel better. My go to phrase is "I'm sorry I hurt your feelings. We just can't draw on the walls. Would you like a hug?" I'd say this when I was letting them out of time out. It doesn't get them out of the consequence, but it does let them know that you understand that their feelings were hurt, and you apologize for that part.

This also goes for taking in a manner to your children that is rude or mean. Some parents do this out of frustration, while others may do it because that was how their parents spoke to them. I cringe when I hear someone in the store yelling and cursing at their child that is still in diapers. I cringe whether the child is small or not. When we say negative things to our children, that becomes their internal monologue. That's what they hear on repeat all through childhood, and then it follows them into adulthood, and every relationship they have. Hearing you're stupid, or you always mess things up makes for low self-esteem and low self-worth.

You could have said it out of frustration, and that isn't normally how you speak to your child, but in that moment, you broke. You have just given them permission to do the same to themselves, and to other people. Can you fix it if you've already said something harmful? I'm sure you can, but the best way to fix a bad experience like that is to not repeat it. Apologize as soon as you come to the realization that you were wrong, and then don't do it again. I know this section of this brief chapter is not for everyone. Some people may be horrified that people would ever dare to talk to their children that way, while others may be just coming to the realization that their behavior is not normal. No matter which parent you are, it's OK. Today is a new day, and new behaviors can become a pattern to establish positive memories and words of affirmation for your child.

This concept also goes for what we expose our children to outside of our own behaviors. Maybe your spouse or significant other is verbally or physically abusive. Maybe they call you names. Maybe your friend comes over and smokes pot on your porch when they visit you. Your child is absorbing what they see. They are absorbing what you allow to happen to you, and around you. They are looking to you for your judgement. How are they supposed to make good choices later in life if you're making poor choices in front of them now. They notice and absorb all the information that is presented to them, or in front of them.

If you wouldn't want your child to either become an abuser, or be abused, consider seeking help for your relationship if it's not safe. If you wouldn't want your child to be spoken down to, reconsider what you allow to be said to you. If you wouldn't want your child to hang around people that abuse drugs, consider who you are exposing them to. Children will do what they see. I said it earlier, and I'll say it again. They do what they see, and they accept what you allow yourself to accept. If you want different for your child, show them something different.

It is so amazing to me what our little guys can comprehend, and what their brains can protect them from. Establish those positive behaviors now. Don't let their internal monologue be of you yelling at them or you telling them their shortcomings on repeat. That's heavy stuff you guys. Our words are so powerful. We must speak life into our children. We must help them find their strong characteristics and nurture them. Teach them to be proud of themselves. Teach them to be confident. Confidence starts at home. Have you ever met an adult who wasn't confident? Maybe you're an adult that isn't confident. Try to think about where that may come from.

It never dawned on me that everyone didn't grow up confident until I was much older. We may have been fairly poor growing up, but my mom and dad spoke life into us every day. They laid the foundation of confidence at home, so when I was getting bullied at school, it hurt, but it didn't break me because I knew who I was. If I had a different set of parents, or even if my biological dad stayed involved in my life, I'm not sure they kind of confidence I would have had to face it. It wasn't until my dad passed away that I realized what his presence meant to who I was as a person. I quickly found that he was my protective factor, and the reason I felt confident enough to even attempt a reconciled relationship with my biological father. Now that he's gone, my confidence is shaken in that area, but in every other area in my life, what he helped to instill is there and flourishing.

My siblings are helpful. My siblings are loving. My siblings are extremely family oriented. My siblings speak love and life into their children. We are this way because of what we saw as children. We love with our whole hearts, and speak to the ones we love gently, because it's what was shown to us. There are so many broken people in this world. So many people that are damaged by their childhoods. So many lost children walking around in these adult bodies trying to figure out a way to repair themselves from their childhoods. So, I implore you, that if you have ever spoken to your children in a negative way, please apologize to them, and consistently show them that you don't feel that way about them. Immerse them with love. I know, this was more serious than my other chapters, but it's for good reason. We have got to show our children the proper way to behave through our own actions and words, so we can put good people out into the world.

I want you to ask yourself what you're doing right now to raise good humans. If you don't like the answer I encourage you to look at the parts that you can change. If you find things you can change, change them. If you can't find things that you can change, you're not looking hard enough. I know even I can change a few things to make more of an effort to put more good out into the world through my children. I hope that everyone can find something and do what they need to do to address the issue and change it. If the only thing you can think of is being in an unsafe situation, again, seek help. You deserve better and so do your children.

12

They're Children

Such a strange title. You may be thinking, it's a parenting book, of course we are talking about children. Yes, yes, we are. And quite honestly, I'm not sure I can even pull a full chapter out of this, but I'm darned sure going to give it a try. Our children are not our friends. They aren't. They aren't our friends as infants, and they aren't our friends as teenagers. They aren't even our friends for any of the ages in between infant and teenager. Crazy concept, right?! Well recently I had a friend come to me for advice on what to do about their spouse talking to their child as an adult. As in confiding in a child, and speaking negatively about other adults, including my friend to their child. How do you handle that? I certainly couldn't tell my friend to run from their spouse, though I wanted to. Not because I think their spouse is awful, but because the behavior of treating your child, young child at that, as an adult is just not something that should be done. Children are children. We cannot give them the weight of an adult world because we need a friend. If you need someone to talk with, confide in a sister, a friend, a therapist, a pastor. Confide in anyone other than your child.

First, let me just tell you that this happens more often than anyone would like to believe. I honestly don't believe that parents are doing this on purpose. I think parents may be frustrated, or lonely, and just think of their children as someone they can talk to. Children are forgiving, and they will listen because they don't know any better, but if you're telling your kids about your personal problems, I'd encourage you to stop. This can be very confusing for children and can contribute to their misbehavior. If a child is being treated as an adult the information could be too much for them, which may cause them to act out. They could also begin to believe that the rules don't apply to them because you're speaking with them like they are aiding in paying the mortgage. Imagine the immense pressure you are placing on them by forcing them to interact with you as an adult.

This also goes for giving little ones too much responsibility. Again, some parents do this without even having the realization that they are doing so. This is something that tends to happen to first born children, and it's easy to do because they're little helpers. We should certainly encourage them to be helpful with their younger sibling, but we shouldn't expect for them to take on a good portion of responsibility in helping take care of them. Children want to help, and they want to please their parents, but sometimes it gets mixed up. The first-born child can carry the weight of being like a second parent, even as young as four years old. It's one thing to ask them to fetch a diaper. It's another thing entirely for you to expect them to watch their sibling while you shower, and they are in complete charge of an infant or younger sibling, when they are barely in charge of their own actions. I've seen parent become angry when they've told their preschooler to look after a younger sibling, and then that sibling gets hurt, or does something they aren't supposed to. The child gets scolded with "I told you to watch your brother" or "you were supposed to be watching them." I've even seen people punish their oldest child for things their youngest child did, because the older sibling wasn't watching them.

I'm not saying you can never shower if you're a stay at home parent. Of course, your child can help, so you can get things done. I'm saying they shouldn't be expected to do so in a manner that you would expect from a responsible adult. If you need one sibling to keep an eye on the other while you cook dinner, or hop in the shower, try to do it at nap time. Or, when the younger sibling is napping, so the only thing the older one has to do is let you know when the younger one wakes up. If that just doesn't work, placing the infant in a playpen, and removing things they shouldn't play with for the few minutes you'll be out of the room could work. When I need to do something that requires me to walk out of the room, I make sure the room is closed off with gates, and there's nothing in the reach of the baby. Now, my children are much older than preschoolers, and I do give them more responsibility for their younger sibling, but when they were toddlers and preschoolers, nap time is when I got things done.

Naptime can be your friend, which is why it's so important to get your little one on a schedule. During naptime you can prep dinner, cook lunch, shower, clean, or walk to the mailbox. I know endless possibilities within the confines of your property (insert sarcastic tone here). The point is, this frees up some of your physical and mental space. When my older children are at school, in order to go to the bathroom, or get ready to leave the house, my bathtub turns into a playpen. Yeah, you heard me. If you haven't tried this hack, you should get on it. I can get so much done and get ready so much faster when I throw some toys in the bathtub and put my youngest in there. I can see what he's doing from the mirror, and he's not in any danger of seriously injuring himself. Now, if your little guy can climb out of the bathtub, then this hack isn't for you, but if they can't, totally give this a try. It is so hard to try to fix your hair, or your makeup with a baby on your hip, or pulling on your pant leg. So, grab some of their favorite toys and put them in an empty bathtub. My little guy thinks its deliriously fun. Though, I'm not sure why. They're the same toys that were on the living room floor.

I didn't write this chapter to sound judgy or be judgy. I know there are some people out there that absolutely have to utilize their children for free or cheap labor when it comes to child care. I know that's a thing. I'm writing this chapter as my 19-year-old is acting as my nanny to my 1 year old because of the astronomical cost of child care. I'm writing about treating children as adults because it happens and it's unfortunate when we give them things to handle that they are not yet equipped to do.

When children are given such a big role, such as confidant, or caregiver before they are able to handle that role, they can become resentful. Resentment turns into unwanted behaviors, which turns into frustration for the parent. Should our children be given responsibilities? Absolutely. They simply need to be age appropriate. Your five-year-old can watch your infant or toddler while they're in a confined place like a play yard, while you go to the bathroom, or cook a quick meal. That's a few minutes, and you've done your due diligence to make sure there was nothing harmful in the room for either of them to get to, and the youngest was secured in a confined space that wouldn't allow for them to sneakily eat something off of the floor. You are doing the best you can, so I don't want this chapter to feel in the least bit judgy. I just want to give you something to think about if you're a parent that gives hefty responsibilities to your little one.

13

The Controversy of Don't

I was not going to include this chapter in my book. Quite honestly, I thought it was silly and unrealistic, but my friend made a compelling argument for why people shouldn't say don't to their children. Well, not so much compelling as in I now believe people shouldn't say don't to their children, but compelling as in I understand the confusion behind people believing they shouldn't say it. First of all, I want to say it is completely unrealistic. It just is. People are going to say don't when speaking to children. Their brains can process the word. There are no scholarly articles supporting that little brains cannot process the "nt" on the end of don't, which in turn makes them believe they *should* do the thing you are telling them not to do. I mean, I looked. I looked for a few days and could not find a darned thing that supported her argument, but I did find some blog posts about the topic. The posts didn't site their sources to confirm their theory, so I have to assume this is something they heard from someone else, or they made it up.

Are you questioning why I decided to put this in the book if I just laid out in the first paragraph why I shouldn't have included it? Look at you being all impatient. I wanted to explore how this came about, and by reading several blog posts and scholarly articles, it seems that there is just a misconception of the use of the word. So, from what I gather, people are confusing the use of the word don't, with articles and research surrounding using positive reframing. Using positive reframing is always a good idea, and if you do it enough will become second nature. When my friend was making her argument for not using the word don't, she used the anecdote of a child running out into the street and the parent saying, "don't run into the street" vs. "stay in the yard." My initial response was, if a child is running into the street, you should not be parenting from afar in that situation.

You should be actively removing the child, stopping them from going into the street, while simultaneously saying we don't run into the street, or we play in the yard. I don't know, maybe I just don't have enough personal discipline to constantly use positive reframing when it comes to dangerous situations. Maybe I'm just realistic when it comes to parents remembering to use a positive reframe in times of danger. I'm not really sure which it is, but I'm going to venture the guess that it's probably both.

I get it, throughout this book I give you things you can do to change your child's behavior, and many of those things require you to change your behavior, or the way you speak to your child in order to alter their behavior to a more acceptable outcome. But, I wouldn't tell you to do something that I wouldn't do, or something I felt was unrealistic and wouldn't be followed anyway. If I told you something that was difficult to follow, that would be a waste of paper. You can certainly try to avoid saying don't to your child, but the world won't. Your children will hear the word don't the majority of their lives, and they'll hear the word no, more often than that. We cannot protect them from hearing something negative, which I don't believe that the word don't is a damaging negative term. It's part of the English language, and they'll hear it outside of your home.

Positively reframing things is a wonderful concept and is certainly possible when the situation is not in relation to immediate danger. When the situation allows for you to process a way to use positive reframing, use it. We went over it a little when we were talking about strong characteristics in your child that you might have the urge to snuff out. I know it was a few chapters ago, but do you remember how we reframed using the word "bossy" to saying they're "direct?" Those are positive reframes, and they should absolutely be used when appropriate. If your child is about to run into the street, for the love of snickerdoodles and apple juice, go get them! That is not the time to process a positive reframe. That is not the time to parent from a distance. That is not the time to reach for your handy parenting book to see how you should handle the situation. That is the time for action.

In this conversation with my friend we also discussed the word no, and how some parents are also avoiding the use of the word. My cousin tried this. This was many years ago, maybe 12, but she insisted that she was not going to use the word no when speaking to her child. At the time her child was maybe a year or so old. She was old enough to walk around and get into stuff. She had great intentions and purpose for not wanting to use the word. It was because she wanted her child to know that she could do anything, and she didn't want to be the first person to tell her child no, possibly damaging her self-esteem. Well, talking to my cousin now, it's like the no factory at her house. You know that commercial for Luvs. Any time new parents make these grandiose plans for how they are going to raise their children, and I know they will be very difficult, if not impossible to carry out in the long term, I always think of that commercial. "You live, you learn, and then you get Luvs." There is no truer sentiment when it comes to parenting.

Each of you children will be parented slightly differently. It's not because you don't love them the same, or your rules become more relaxed. It's because you're more experienced. You know what works and what doesn't. You're also more flexible to what might work for that particular child, because you've likely found out that your children are very different from each other and require different approaches. Your core parenting style and principal will not change, but the smaller things will. You may find that time outs don't work for Jacob like they did for Lucy, but positive rewards work well. You may figure out that none of it works, and you want to throw the whole kid away, and start again. Don't do that. Something works. My sister used to feel this way, but when I dug a little deeper, it was that she wasn't using one type of consequence consistently enough. She would try time outs for a week or two, and then jump to restrictions, and when that didn't work, she would jump to something else for a week. Whatever your choices for your child, the key to it working will always be consistency.

If you choose to go the route of not using don't or no when speaking to your child, just know that in order for it to have the greatest impact, you have to be consistent. Also, be aware that someone else is going to say those words to your child. It doesn't mean your children are going to have a breakdown because they heard the word don't for the first time. I mean, well, they may have a breakdown, but they'll get over it because don't is not a malicious word. Our job as parents is to prepare our children for the real world.

So, if you're replacing don't and no, make sure your kids understand that they are going to hear it from other people, and make sure they understand what it means. There are going to be people that love them that tell them no. There are going to be people that love them that tell them don't. You may give up on the noble mission of not using those words when speaking to your children and I just want you to know that's fine. However, you turn out parenting your children is fine. Of course, I want you to parent in the least stressful was as possible, so I hope you can learn from this book, but I don't want you doing something that feels unnatural, and counterproductive to how you'd like your children to be raised.

I'm not sure if this is really a controversy, but I do know that I was shocked to learn how some parents interpreted it. I included it in this book for the parents that read these things on social media and instantly think they have been parenting all wrong. This is not the first time I've heard of not using don't, but it's the first time I heard it come out of someone's mouth. I usually see a meme, or some sort of graphic on social media from some blogger with a list of things we should say instead of words and phrases that have a "negative connotation." This is not to discount bloggers. I blog. I love my fellow blogging mamas out there, but not all bloggers are created equal when it comes to their fund of knowledge. Mom bloggers have a huge spectrum of parenting techniques, and many mom bloggers don't even mention how they parent. The ones that do talk about how they parent are typically struggling through the process like most other parents out there, which is the very thing that makes them relatable and grabbing the attention of the masses. This does not discredit their ability to parent, but it also doesn't mean they're a voice of authority in the parenting community. Take their advice with a grain of salt.

Again, this is not to discredit whatever blogger that graphic came from. They sound like they're a wonderful parent. I mean, they have dedicated themselves to not saying no, and don't to their children. They're probably killing the parenting game. Or their children are running amuck and they give preachy advice on Facebook because it makes them feel better. Either way, no concern of mine. I don't even tell my friends anything about raising their children. When they ask me, I tell them what works for my child. I don't give them professional parenting advice unless they specifically ask. They rarely specifically ask. Parents don't want to know or feel as if they're doing everything wrong when it comes to their child rearing abilities, so they avoid asking an expert. I don't want to isolate myself, or make my friends feel badly, which I would never do, but you can't control how people will perceive your statements, especially if they're in a defeated headspace. When I do intervene at their request, which is super rare, I typically ask questions. I don't preach at them. I don't make them feel bad. I don't tell them they're doing it wrong. I answer their question with a question because I've found this is the least threatening approach.

When my assistance is requested someone might say, "I really don't understand why John is doing XYZ. I can't get him to listen. What should I do, because he's driving me crazy?" My advice usually sounds like, "How long has he been doing this? Is this a new behavior? Have you tried XYZ?" Most times they haven't tried what I have suggested, so it feels like I've given advice, but I didn't. I just gave them a realistic suggestion on what they could try. Most times, the behavior they are describing is not new behavior, and I noticed it a while ago, but I let my friends be the parents they were meant to be. Can you imagine how annoying and frustrating it would be if your friend the "parenting expert" went behind you telling you all the things you're presumably doing wrong because they keep giving you unsolicited advice.

So, yeah...my friend's children could be little minions from the underworld, and I wouldn't say anything. I would love them, and their parents just like they were well behaved angels. I won't make them feel badly because they're still trying to figure out what works best for their children. So, when I first saw that graphic floating around my timeline, I kept my mouth shut. I think it's a fantastic idea. I just don't feel like it's realistic, but if my friends want to give it the old college try, who am I to deflate their little red balloon? That would be mean and unnecessary. I'm sure if they've supported me and bought this book, they now know how I feel about it. Sorry guys. I love you and now you know why I didn't like, comment or reshare that image.

To recap. You do you when it comes to figuring out if this method is right for you. This is not a subject that is bad or good. It's simply another way to approach this messy thing we call parenting. Your children will not grow up to be resentful because you told them no more times than the law allows. Same goes for if you choose to never tell them no, or don't. Using or not using these two "negative" words is not going to damage their little baby psyches. So, figure out what feels right to you about this topic and use it.

14
What You Say Matters

Feeding off of the last chapter, what you do say to your children matters. It also matters how you say things. Now, I'm not going to become the language police, but as I mentioned before, I come from a family who said "do as I say, not as I do" for most of my childhood. It wasn't even an option to have what was said explained to me. This is something I notice is different across different cultures. Some cultures, like my own think that they shouldn't have to explain what was going on, or why anything was happening to a child. The phrases, "a child is to be seen, and not heard" and "stay in a child's place" are things I heard all the time. Especially when I asked questions. Other cultures embrace their children's questions and have no problem explaining the why of things to their children. And I assume there are likely some cultures in the middle of the spectrum. What is your style when it comes to explaining things to your kids? Do you shut them down, or do you indulge in their questioning?

Children are natural scientist and explorers. They love an explanation to things, and they love knowing things. I find that some parents either, intentionally or unintentionally talk down to their children as if they are unintelligent, or some sort of annoyance. Yeah, kids can be annoying at times, but telling them they're annoying you instead of acting like their existence is an annoyance to your life would be a better alternative. Kids are not opposed to honesty. But it does hurt their feelings when you talk to them like they don't matter, just as it would hurt your feelings if someone you loved did the same thing. Just because you're an adult, doesn't mean you're smarter than a child. You may be older, and you may have more experiences, but that doesn't mean that you're above that child. I've seen this time and time again, and if I'm being completely honest, it hurts my heart.

You cannot raise children who are respectful if you're being disrespectful. Speaking down to your child is disrespectful. Telling your child "because I said so" or "because I'm the adult and you're not" all the time isn't respectful. Sure, if it's a surprise and you don't want them to know, then "because I said so" may be the best option, but when it comes to everyday instances, try to give them a better answer. Here's the thing about children. They don't ask for more information than they can handle. If they ask you why, or what's wrong, or anything along those lines - tell them! Tell them using their age as a guide. Don't over explain. If they want more information, they will ask for it. If they're asking the question, they are ready for the answer.

Parents get caught up on this with big topics. Topics like sex, drugs, or where babies come from, often causes parents to have the deer in headlights look. If your child is asking you about sex, chances are they've heard the term before. You're not doing them any favors or protecting them from anything by avoiding the question, or worse, telling them it's none of their business because they're children. Explain it in a developmentally appropriate way. Same goes for drugs and where babies come from. Let's be realistic here for a minute. We are talking about toddler and preschoolers in this book. Unless they're being exposed to something through TV or family members that have some issues going on, they won't be asking about anything but where babies come from.

Preschoolers love this question. Parents love to avoid this question. I'm not sure why parents don't want to give an honest answer to this particular question. I would think that this question has been around since the beginning of people. I'm sure Jesus asked Mary and Joseph where babies came from, and the children that were here before Jesus asked their parents. This question and answer should be perfected after the thousands of years that people have been on this earth. I'm almost positive animals likely have some version of this question in the animal kingdom. Especially those chimps that can sign.

I'm getting off on a weird tangent about Jesus and chimps. Let's bring it back. If your child is asking you where babies come from. Tell them the truth. Don't get into sperm and ovaries, they don't know what that is. They don't need to know a baby is a zygote before becoming a fetus. They don't need to know about menstrual cycles and ovulation. They're 4, not 13. They need to know the very basics that are developmentally and age appropriate. Children ask different variations of this question, and it seems that no matter the way the question is asked, most parents responses are the same.

"Mommy, where do babies come from?' Or "Mommy, how did brother get in your tummy?" It's the same question. They aren't asking about sex. They're asking how and why there's a tiny human inside of another human. Don't tell them you swallowed a watermelon seed. Don't tell them you don't know. Don't tell them a stork brought the baby. You're doing them a disadvantage and lying to your child. How do you answer the question? Here's a simple way to answer without getting into details. "When a mommy and daddy love each other, they lay down together to try to make a baby. Sometimes it works, and then the baby grows in mommy's tummy." Now, this answer was not good enough for my daughter. She asked, "but how do you make a baby" and followed up with "how does the baby get out."

The cool thing about kids, is when they are done learning because they feel like you gave them an adequate answer, they just leave. They say "OK" and go back to playing or watching Paw Patrol. I think this is where parents overthink things and believe they have to go into great detail. I'm sure you're wondering what on earth I said to my 4-year-old daughter when she asked those questions.

Well here goes. I told her "mommy has a baby maker on the inside, and daddy has a baby maker on the outside. In order for mommy and daddy to make a baby, they have to put their baby makers together for a little while, and then 9 months later a baby comes out." Of course, she followed up with the "how does the baby get out" question. I did something radical and told her the truth. At the time, she called her vagina her "self," and to be quite honest, I'm not sure where she got that. I've always told my children the proper names for their body parts. She was probably the only kid in her class that knew what a vulva was. Anyway, I told her "most of the time, babies come out of your vagina, but sometimes doctors have to get them out through your tummy." You know what she said? "Oh. Can I have a snack?"

The whole conversation lasted less than two minutes. So, if you're worried about being uncomfortable, don't. Your discomfort will be brief. Your child's attention span is short. The more you avoid the tough questions, the more they're going to ask them. This is also where I talk about opening up the communication now. People always want to know why my kids aren't afraid or embarrassed to talk to me about sex. This is why. We've been talking about sex all their lives. They know I won't shy away from the hard questions, and I'll give them the truth. They know I won't judge them, but I'll tell them what I expect.

They know I'm here for them if someone is giving them misinformation, which is typical in middle and high school. Yes, my 13-year-old came to me and told me about his very first hug from his girlfriend. Yes, my daughter told me about her very first kiss from her boyfriend when she was 15. Yes, my now 11-year-old told me about someone he thought was pretty when he was 9. They tell me these things because we have open communication.

My kids aren't out there having sex at an early age, because they know about it. If anything, the more educated your child is about sex, the more likely they are to wait until they're developmentally ready to have it. I wanted my children to have the truth, and to be treated as autonomous people. They have body autonomy, meaning they are in control of their own bodies. Their bodies do not belong to me. Their bodies belong to them, and them alone. Their worth is not tied up in their virginity, or how many sexual partners they will have in a lifetime.

Talk to your kids. Talk to them early. Talk to them often. My kids' friends know that we are open about sex. Their parents know it too. In fact, I would gather that their parents probably allow them to come over because they know they are going to hear about sex and can, and *do* ask their questions to me, and I give them honest answers. My children are good kids. They are informed kids. They don't judge other kids for their actions, but they do talk to me about it and ask questions about what they should do, or if they should say something to their friend. Talk to your kids guys. Talk to them like they are full people. Not adults, but full people.

Talk to them as often as they can stand it. Give them room to ask the tough questions and be brave enough to give them the answers. If you aren't sure how to have these conversations, I would suggest talking to them in the car. Something about not having to make eye contact opens the communication right up. Talk to them while you're cooking or cleaning. Again, the eye contact thing. Don't sit them down to have this big grand talk like they do on TV.

The only thing you will accomplish with this approach is them being extremely uncomfortable, and you being uncomfortable. Talk to them little by little starting as early as they can talk. Starting with giving their private parts a name. Starting with answering their dang questions like you respect the time and thought process it took for them to verbalize what they wanted to say.

Through the early years of their life, you are their Google. They get the majority of their information from the way you behave, and what you say. No one has the level of influence over a child's behavior, like a parent. So, I urge you to be kind in front of them, be kind when speaking to them, and be kind when answering their questions. The way you treat people, will be the way your children treat people. When they get older, they default to what they were taught while growing up, so show kindness to them and in front of them.

15

Sibling Rivalry

I have only experienced this with my boys. I have three of them, so it's fun. For the longest time, they were best buddies, but when they were toddlers, I wasn't sure they would both survive. My oldest boys are 2.5 years apart. I thought that was a good distance, so I really wasn't prepared for the sibling rivalry that started when the youngest of the two turned about 10 months old. He would get so upset when I showed my oldest son any attention.

There was one day that I remember distinctly where my then 3-year-old sat next to me on the edge of the bed and I snuggled him while we watched TV for a few minutes. About five seconds after we got comfy, my other son crawls off of my lap and behind my other son, then begins kicking him as fast and as hard as he possibly could. I picked him up and corrected the behavior, then a few minutes later he was at it again.

This was my first experience with any sort of sibling rivalry as a mom. My oldest child, my daughter, didn't argue or fight with anyone. Maybe it was because she was five years older, or maybe it was because she was the only girl. I don't know, but I was not prepared. Keeping with my trend of honesty with you guys, we really didn't cover this in school. We went over every age and stage of a single child in depth. We went over the psychology of a child's behavior in depth. I mean, I had whole classes on the psychology behind a child's behavior. They were some of my favorite classes, but when it came to sibling rivalry, we glossed over it, so I guess it didn't stick.

So, here I was with these two boys that suddenly can't stand each other, which confused the mess out of me, because the one starting most of the issues was the toddler. I was flying solo. Flying without instructions. Flying by the seat of my pants. I was stumped on how to handle this situation for the first time in my parenting career. I realize that most parents are stumped for much of their child's childhood, so I don't say this to be facetious, it's just the truth.

Now, I grew up with a lot of siblings, and we fought often. My brother actually stood in the middle of a hill to hit me in the head with a bat while I rode down the hill on a Big Wheel. It was his Big Wheel, and I stole it while he was riding it. I more than just stole it. I pushed him off of it while he was in the middle of riding it, and then ran up the hill to ride it down. He had every right to be mad. It just looked like he was having so much fun riding down the hill, and he wouldn't share.

At the time, I didn't have a Big Wheel...I was too big for one. I believe at the time, I was 10 and he was 5. In this situation, I was the one that should've known better. And before you get your panties in a wad, you should know it was 1990. Parent's parented differently back then. We played outside for hours without adult supervision, and this was obviously a time where we weren't being supervised.

Sometimes I wonder how we even survived childhood in the 80's and 90's. We were left to our own devices much more often than not. It helped build character and self-sufficiency, but we probably could've been kidnapped or worse. During this time when I was being hit in the head with a metal bat...did I mention it was a metal bat earlier? It was metal. My older brother played baseball, so he had several aluminum bats laying around. So, yeah, I got hit in the head with a bat when I was supposed to be watching my brother. I was not really watching him. I mean, I made sure he didn't run into the street, and that no creepy person jumped out and grabbed him, but I really wasn't watching him like a responsible person. Probably because I was a child. I spent the better part of the afternoon antagonizing him, and then pretending I wasn't antagonizing him when an adult came out to check. When my older brother was in charge, he antagonized both of us. It was the circle of life, man. Just living the dream.

My childhood was my only experience I had to draw on when it came to sibling rivalry, and if I was drawing on that, the outlook was grim. Though, my brothers and I got along well for the most part, we found different ways to torture each other when we got bored. And most times boredom was the only reason we had to harass each other. Well, that, and they liked to believe I was "the golden child." They still call me that on occasion. I was the only girl for a long time, and they felt like I couldn't do anything wrong in our parent's eyes. I didn't believe them, but as I got older, I did notice a pattern of me getting away with things that they never could have. I used it to my advantage as another way to get under their skin. I was an awful child. I mean, in the grand scheme of things I was a very good child that always followed the rules, but I was awful to my brothers. Just awful. I'm surprised I didn't get beat up more often by them.

Reminiscing on my childhood, made me realize I should probably get advice from my mom to help me deal with my boys, and now I can pass that along to you. My mom had five children. Five. I'm sure when we were fighting she wished she would've stopped at none. My mom's advice was simple. She said treat sibling rivalry like you would treat any other behavior. What? How could I do this when every day it was the battle between Mufasa and Scar in my house? She made it sound so simple. Treat it like I would any other unwanted behavior.

I guess in my frustration, I hadn't even begun to think about sibling rivalry as an unwanted behavior. I thought of it more like not getting along, and me trying to force them to do so. When I approached it from a typical behavior issue stance, things began to change. Was the change overnight? Absolutely not, but a change did come. I was passing out time outs like they were free stickers. I was also rewarding the positive interactions between them. "You guys are playing so well together. Let's go to the park." They loved the rewards for good behavior, so they behaved better more often. The fighting began to decrease significantly.

By the time my younger boy was 2 and my older one was 5, they didn't fight at all. They talked things out and negotiated when they both wanted the same thing. If you don't think a two-year-old can negotiate, you would be wrong. Depending on their vocabulary and the stage in development they're in, they can be fairly good at expressing their needs.

Not all two-year-olds will be able to do this, but some of them certainly can. Once we got the sibling rivalry under control, my house was peaceful, and no longer resembled a scene from The Lion King, I was able to better address my friend's same issues with sibling rivalry. I felt confident that I understood how to handle the issue. There will be some rivalry that is based in favoritism, and the favoritism will need to be addressed first. Most parents don't even realize they are showing favoritism with their children but listen to your kids.

If a common theme is occurring around so and so being the favorite, or getting more, or being able to do more, maybe you need to take a step back. If you still can't see it. Ask a friend if you have a favorite child. Ask an honest friend, not the friend that is going to tell you what you want to hear. We all have at least one truly honest friend, that will let you know the thing that everyone else is afraid to say. Ask them if you have a favorite child. If they point out that you do, in fact have a favorite child. Do your best to remedy the situation. If the answer would be no for one, then make the answer no for both.

Think of it from the other child's perspective. When interacting with your "favorite" child, ask yourself if that's the same way you would interact with the other. Again, most parents don't even realize it, and if someone points it out, they will deny it until the next ice age comes around. If you can figure out the root of sibling rivalry, you can figure out the solution. I can now see how the perception of one sibling being the favorite over the other could be damaging to the other child's self-esteem, and the sibling relationship. Helping your child navigate this time by identifying where the issue lies and working to fix it with the child can be an extremely positive and validating experience for the child. For me, my youngest son was used to being the baby, so when I showed my other son any affection, he saw red. We had a lot of conversations about sharing mommy's attention. With corrective action for the parent as well as the child, and difficult conversations to help identify the problem, sibling rivalry can be properly addressed.

Be patient but be consistent. Children are in desperate need of consistency and proper boundaries. It's amazing to me that even after all of these years, my brothers still view me as the favorite. Our relationships are pretty solid, and now I feel like it's just a teasing thing, and not an actual belief that I am the favorite. We still harass each other, but I don't know siblings that don't. It's not physical, obviously, but every sibling group will have their own silly, still childlike relationships in one way or another.

16

Mommy Needs a Mimosa

I said mimosa, not Momoa. Calm down ladies. Although Jason Momoa would be nice, that wish is not in my realm of possibilities in this book. This chapter is for every parent, but especially the parents that are the default caregiver for their children and more often than not, their spouse. Take a break. Seriously. You need a break. If your break includes a mimosa, or binging any and everything Jason Moma was in, you deserve every single solitary minute of that break.

So many times, we get so wrapped up in taking care of everyone else, that we forget about ourselves. Did I pack their lunch? Did I sign that permission slip? Did I remind the husband about his dentist appointment? Oh no, I forgot the dog needed to go to the vet to renew his flea prescription! Tomorrow's my mom's birthday, I need to remember to pick up a gift. You are doing so much mental exercise every second of every day, and you rarely let on that you might need some help, or even a few uninterrupted minutes to yourself. But, let me tell you, as a mental health specialist, you need to share the load. You need to take a break. It is not only good for your mental health, it's good for your physical health, and good for your relationships.

Don't look at these words like I'm talking crazy. I see your wheels turning, doing more mental acrobats trying to figure out how taking a break is even a possible suggestion. Stop it. More likely than not, you did not make those children by yourself. If you have a spouse, or an ex-spouse, share the load. These are fully grown adults that became adults likely before they met you. They know how to schedule appointments. I bet they can even navigate car rider lane without you telling them step by step how to do it.

They are capable. And if they aren't capable, how on earth did they survive before they met you? They did survive right? I assume they did because you met and married them. I want you to make a list of everything you do in a day. Yeah, I know it's long. Make the list anyway. I'm not timing you. Take as long as you need. Make your list and look at all the things that don't require you to do them. Look at each item on this list and ask yourself is this something that can be delegated. You will find some things that you consider to be non-negotiables, which is great. Put a star next to the non-negotiable items that you *want* to do. For me, my non-negotiable is school drop off. I'm not going to cry if I can't do school drop off, but I'd much prefer me be the one to do it. Same goes for school pick up. Those are non-negotiable.

I have several non-negotiables that allow me to do the things I love to do as a mom but have also delegated a lot of responsibilities. I couldn't do it all. No one can, and if you think your friend Jessica who has 3 kids, a hoity toity job in the city, and a GQ model for a husband is doing it all because she doesn't post her struggles on

Facebook. You would be mistaken. She's not doing it all. No one is. She is getting help from someone. Maybe it's through her husband who picks the kids and takes them to practices. Maybe she has a nanny or a mother's helper. Maybe her own mother is helping. I'm not sure why women lie about things like this, it just makes everyone else feel bad. I started delegating things when I was in grad school. I didn't go to grad school until 8 years after completing my undergrad, so I was an older student. I was working full time in the mental health industry, repairing parent's relationships with their children, and addressing children's problematic behavior. I went to one of the top Catholic universities in the world. And if anyone has gone to any Catholic school, ever, you know they are overachievers when it comes to education.

This was the most stressful and intense program I've ever even thought about going to. During my foundation year, I had to add a 15 hour a week internship on top of working 40 hours a week at my full-time job, navigate my kid's sports and schoolwork, navigate my own school work, and still somehow manage to stay married. My house was a mess. My brain was a mess. I broke. I was trying so hard to do everything that I was forgetting about myself. Being the natural overachiever, and with the media pushing me to believe women could have everything, I feel into the trap.

I remember very distinctly, calling my dad hyperventilating crying as soon as he picked up and asked the magic question "what's wrong?" I couldn't breathe. I couldn't stop crying. I couldn't get myself together. If you have a dad, you know that they automatically go into fix it mode, and I couldn't verbalize what it was that he could fix. My dad, being a dad, said "here, talk to your mother" when he couldn't calm me down. I heard my mom's voice, always steady, always calm. She asked me what was wrong. Explained in a loving manner and tone that she couldn't help if she couldn't understand me. My mom instantly turned back into mommy mode. She told me to take my time, and cry as long as I need to, and she would still be on the other end when I was ready to start talking. I cried for a few more minutes, trying to catch my breath and gather my thoughts to speak in a coherent fashion. I honestly thought my husband was going to have to commit me for excessive crying. I know that's not a thing, but when you have anxiety, and taking the world onto your shoulders, you think all sorts of things. I talked to my mom for what seemed like forever. She calmed me down. She told me what I needed to hear, but I didn't hear her. Her calm and steady voice was great for snapping me back to reality, but even after I was calm, my brain was still in overdrive. When my dad got back on the phone, he was more stern. Still loving, but stern. He told me I scared him, and to call my mom the next time I'm in the midst of a breakdown because he didn't know what to do. He also repeated what my mom said, but in a dad voice.

"Those kids are old enough to help. You shouldn't be doing it all. Tell your husband what you need. You are not superwoman. It's OK to ask for help. Just ask. People will help you." You guys, I scared my parents so badly that they offered to move to where I was to be there for me while I finished my degree. My parents are awesome. I heard my dad. I heard him, and I asked for help. I went back to what I knew to work for the kids. A chore chart when up alongside an RRC chart. I taught them how to use the washer and dryer. My husband showed the boys, (8 and 10 ½ at the time) how to use the dishwasher. Once the chores were more evenly distributed, and I delegated some duties to my husband, I was able to focus more on quality time with my kids when I had it, instead of running around trying to clean after working a 60-hour week and completing school work. As the kids have gotten older, they have started helping out even more, especially since the baby came. Not because I asked, but because they see when something needs to be done, and they do it. Same goes for my husband. Our house is more in sync now, and more peaceful than ever, because everyone is pitching in without being asked, and I have learned to not try to take on the world without asking for a little help.

So, believe me when I say, I'm not telling you to do something that I wouldn't do myself. When people ask me how I do it all; and it's usually friends that only see me through the lense of social media...When they ask, I tell them the truth. I don't do it all. I ask for help and I delegate duties. I find time in the day for myself, and I practice self-care. I'm sure you've heard that term a million times by now. It is such a wonderful concept, and as I've just said, I wholeheartedly take advantage of it. What you don't know about self-care is, it only works if you've got the help.

You can't self-care your way out of depression, or superwoman syndrome. There's not enough self-care in the world for that. The only way self-care works is if yours household or entire lifestyle is changed. You can't dedicate two hours every other Saturday for a pedicure with your sister, but still come home to chaos and expect for the self-care to have revitalized your entire life. It doesn't. You'll feel good for a few minutes after you get home, but you're still walking into the fire when your newly pampered feet walk through your front door. Self-care is more than pedicures and mimosas. Self-care is delegating tasks. Self-care is telling your partner you need their help. Self-care is giving your children age appropriate chores to help you out. Self-care is telling your boss you don't return emails or texts after 5pm or on the weekends. Self-care is taking care of your whole self, not just your feet. I think somewhere down the line in this whole self-care movement, we got sidetracked from the actual meaning of self-care.

I know the thought of your husband or children doing chores probably gives you anxiety. Let them do it anyway. Of course, they're not going to fold the laundry just like you. They will fold the towels in squares instead of neatly and tightly folded rectangles, so they fit in the linen closet better. When you see those towels haphazardly folded, smile, and remind them to put everything where it goes, and silently thank the stars above that you didn't have to do it. Here's the thing, they're never going to learn how to it properly if we don't let them try.

Kids are never going to learn to want to help with household chores if we don't delegate to them. Not giving your children chores is doing them a disservice. These are life skills they need to survive on their own. Cooking, cleaning, washing clothes; all things they'll need to do when they move out. You aren't magically imparted with this wisdom and skill when you turn 18. Sometimes it seems much easier to do it yourself because they won't do it the way you do it, and they will whine and complain like you've threatened to cut their legs off. Fight the urge to take over and make them do it anyway. If you need to, sit in the tub with a glass of wine while they're completing their chores. Out of sight, out of mind. Who am I kidding, it'll still be on your mind, but stay in the tub anyway.

The list I told you to make earlier in this chapter? Keep it handy. When you finish reading this chapter put it on your wall where you can see it. Give those duties you can delegate some serious thought. Then, do the unthinkable. Delegate. Delegate until your heart's content. Delegate until the cows come home. Just delegate. Be sure you enlist your partner's help with enforcing chore duties with your children if you have older ones. If you only have younger ones, they can still help. They can help you pick up the toys in their room. They can help pick up toys or paper off of the living room floor. They can throw things away. At first, especially with older children, it's going to seem like more work than it's worth.

You're changing their routine. You're changing their comfort. They are going to moan and complain and buck against the new system you're putting in place. This is where the RRC chart comes in handy. The eye rolling, and grunting should only last a few weeks. They will fall into a pattern of knowing what their chores are and getting them done without much prompting, if any prompting at all.

Just stay consistent, and truly enjoy your mimosa with your sister next week.

17

It's Not Working

I deliberately put this chapter behind the last one because some of you have older children and the previous chapter will likely annoy your children the most. You are going to feel like it's not working. Moms of littles, you're definitely going to feel like things aren't working as soon as you implement a behavior changing method, and we talked about a lot of those earlier in the book. So, here's the deal. Behavior change doesn't happen the way we want it to happen. It's never a smooth transition.

Some of the smaller changes will be smooth, but it will almost always move along a bell curve. If I can figure out how to put a bell curve chart in this book, I'll do it so you can refer back to it. If you don't find it in this chapter, it's because I didn't figure it out. Hey, I'm a social worker, not a computer person. We will get to the description of the bell curve and the actual bell curve (fingers crossed) in a little bit. I want to tell you what to expect when you change something small, like no yelling in the house. They will need reminders, but they're likely to be just fine with this rule. If they're in preschool or daycare, they're likely already used to this rule. You will likely sail right through this change.

The rule they're going to fight you on most is bedtime and electronics. If you've been letting your little one stay up until they fell asleep on their own, they are going to make you feel like the devil for giving them a reasonable bedtime. They are going to fight this from the moment you try to enforce it. They're going to cry. They'll continuously come out of their room. They'll constantly need something, anything. Let me tell you something. Set their routine and keep it that way. They do not need 15 glasses of water. They don't. Unless you want to change their sheets, every night or keep them in diapers until they're double digits.

Make a rule about water. For example, my kid's rule was no water 30 minutes before bed. They are not dehydrated. Most toddlers and preschoolers are hydrated just fine. They drink multiple cups of milk, juice and water a day. They do not suddenly need 7 glasses of water to sleep. Start cuddle time before bedtime. So, when you cut off liquids, make that story and snuggle time. That way, when they are trying to use that to convince you that you don't love them enough because you won't leave the couch or your bed to snuggle with them, you can say, "we had snuggle time, and now it's over. It's time for bed." Be stern but loving, and don't give in. The minute you give in, you've taught them "I just have to ask X amount of times before it works." You have now trained your child to nag you longer.

They won't be psychologically damaged because you won't bend to their every want. You give them hugs and snuggles throughout the day. You've given them frequent access to liquids. You've made sure they used the bathroom or changed their diaper before bed. You've read them a story. They are fine. Children are very resourceful when it comes to getting their needs met. And I say needs with a grain of salt, because they don't *need* any of these things throughout the night, with the exception of an occasional nightmare. These are things they want, and it just feels like a need to them. Be prepared for tears. Be prepared to be unfriended by your preschooler. Be prepared for tantrums. Be prepared to stick it out anyway. Children have a way of hurting your feelings with a single cry. Continue to stick to your guns. They WILL adjust.

The same goes for removing electronics. Setting a timer and keeping them put away when it's not their allotted time is good for their little brains. They don't know that because they're children, and they want what they want, when they want it. It's our job as parents to make the best decisions for them. Children as young as two shouldn't be on an electronic at all. If they are on one, it should be limited to 15 min a day. They're already exposed to TV, because I assume you don't live in the Victorian Era. My TV is on all the time when we are home. Unless you plan on making everyone's, including your own TV time 15 min a day, I expect your little one to be exposed to the big flashing box.

A television constantly on is enough stimulation for a little brain, add in an electronic device that they can control and hold in their hand, and we are looking at the potential to cause major behavioral issues. So, the first few days when you take the electronics away, or limit their use, they are going to likely throw the mother of all fits. Expect fits of hurricane strength for a few days. They are definitely not going to be your friend. This is a good time to remind them that you're their parent, not their friend. They may even do things completely out of character, like hit you, or throw things. Go back to your RRC chart and give them the appropriate consequence. Whatever you do, don't give in. Going to dinner in public? Leave the tablets at home. Do not give in. You may be thinking that this is the only way you *can* eat in public. It's not. Our parents took us out in public without electronics, we all survived and learned how to behave at a casual dining restaurant. The kid's menus have games on them for a reason. If your kids are too little to play the games on the menu as directed, now would be a good time to work on colors or letter recognition. I love the word search puzzles for just that reason. I pick a random letter, tell them what the letter is, and see if they can find it again. They are occupied and quiet, because they're busy looking for the letter "O."

You are going to feel burnt out from excess tantrums, and you'll likely hate me, and think I was lying or playing some cruel trick on you by telling you to do this. I'm not. Raising children is not for the faint. It's much easier to start these habits when they are babies and continue to have firm loving boundaries as they grow, but again, no one leaves the hospital with instructions on how to raise your child and looking in the parenting book section at any local retailer can be overwhelming. There are so many opinion-based books that look like fact. There are many humorous books, that show you that everyone has the same struggles, but they don't really tell you how to address it. Then there are the books by experts that drone on and one about how experty they are, but the information is practically over your head, and it's boring to read. I have yet to find a parenting book that I just love, so I decided to write one. Hopefully I've mixed enough evidenced based parenting information in this book, in a way that is fun to read, and easy to follow.

I want to talk to you about the developmental stages for a bit, and then we will get into the bell curve I brought up earlier. When your toddler starts getting close to two, they start showing they want some independence. They are also usually helpful and want to copy most everything you do, so while they may want to do a few things on their own: taking off their diaper, doing the exact opposite of what you said, or trying to take off their own clothes. They are very moldable to new boundaries. You can thank their gnat like attention spans for that. They don't remember what happened ten minutes ago, so they likely won't realize you're enforcing a new boundary.

Preschoolers are a whole different animal. Their attention span is longer, and they have had years of your current rules and boundaries ingrained in their little minds. It's harder to enforce new boundaries, because they know this is different. They know last week mom let me have my tablet all day, every day, and this week I can't have it at all. They're going to lose their crap.

By this stage in development, they're like tiny teenagers. They think they can do all sorts of things on their own, yup, picking out their own clothes and insisting their shoes are on the right feet are just the tip of the iceberg...they are decision makers. They are questioners of your every decision, and things that aren't even your decision. By now you probably want to scrub the word "why" from the human vocabulary in every language, just to avoid them picking it up from a native tongue different than their own. They also tend to get a little sassy at this point. They think "no" is a suggestion, and they can tell you what to do. As frustrating as all of this independence can be, it's all completely normal. Don't worry, around 6 or 7, they'll go back to being their sweet selves...until the preteen hormones surge. Normal kid again after that. And then the teen hormones surge. Fun times. Fun times.

The thing about all of these stages of development, they all need structure. They don't need you to hover over them for every move they make, they just need practical rules that are consistently enforced, so they can make logical decisions and behave accordingly when they are out of your sight. We have all seen "that kid," and as parents we hope that our kid is not the one other parents and teachers are pointing at as "that kid." Believe me, the parents of that child know they are unruly, and behave like they have little to no home training. Appropriate boundary setting, and logical consequences can help eliminate those unwanted behaviors. Sprinkle in some praise and recognition for positive behaviors, and we've got a winning combination. Eliminating this unruly behavior will be a challenge because your kid is going to challenge you. I mean really, challenging us is what kids do.

Speaking of challenges, let's talk about the bell curve of eliminating a child's behavior, or if you prefer, the bell curve of setting boundaries. It's honestly not just for a child's behavior, it's really anyone's behavior that is being eliminated, but we're talking about children, so I'll try to stay on topic. The bell curve is visual depiction of the elimination of a behavior, or the introduction of a new boundary. What happens is, when you first introduce the new boundary with correlating rewards, or praise, the line is fairly flat because you're coming off of the status quo for their behaviors. The new boundaries are enforced, and the behaviors go up. The more the new boundaries are enforced, the more the behaviors you're trying to eliminate go up, so if you're looking at a graph of this, you would be seeing the top of the hill. You continue to enforce the new boundaries, because you are staying the course, right? So, as you continue to be consistent with enforcing these boundaries, and RRC's, the behaviors start to go down. The behaviors continue to go down until they are eliminated or mostly eliminated, because let's be real, kids have momentary lapses in judgement like any of us.

I tried to do the thing, and it was pretty terrible. Apparently drawing on computer is not my strong suit. I attempted to draw a bell curve that represents what is most likely to happen when you introduce a behavior changing boundary. The bell curve shows a flat line of when the new behavior is introduced, and the line goes up on a slope as the child pushes back against the new system. It peaks, and then goes back down. I wish I could have depicted on for you. If you're confused, just Google a bell curve. It will all make sense then. Draw a copy and stick it in your purse or hang it on your refrigerator. I don't care where you place it as a reminder, just be reminded that the explosion of unwanted behavior is going to come to an end. It will. I promise. Have I lied to you yet? No, I haven't. So, take a deep breath, mama (or daddy), you got this!

18
Sharing Is Not Always Caring

Sharing is something that we as parents say a million times a week. We want our children to share with others, and share with us, and we hope that others return the favor and share with our children. Not sharing can seem like a problematic situation, and often leads to yelling, crying, screaming, and sometimes stomping or hitting. As soon as our child has a negative reaction to sharing, we get embarrassed and upset with our child for not wanting to share their toy. Sharing is not something that happens naturally. You can't expect for a child to want to just share whatever they have without practice, and in their minds, without reason. They don't understand why you're letting some kid take something that they are actively playing with. Nor do they understand why you're making them share toys that they have clearly staked claim to. They want to know why. And if they aren't old enough to ask why, they may really show out behaviorally. This is not their fault. They have a limited vocabulary as toddlers, and as we talked about before, this causes some unwanted behaviors. Little ones, especially early toddlers, don't understand the concept of sharing.

Have you ever made your child share? Eh, most of us have, I don't know why I even asked that question. Let me ask this one. Have you ever made your child share a favorite toy or item? I can't hear you, so I'm going to assume you said yes, even if you didn't. It plays better for the sake of this paragraph. You just made your kid share their favorite thing, and now they're fuming. Well of course they are. It was their very favorite, no one else can even look at it, thing. I have seen this happen more times than not, so stick with me here. Your kid is in full meltdown mode. Did he make a choice in his behavior? Likely not. Your child is now responding to a sacred item being used by someone else.

I suggest coming up with a no share list. These would be items that are either a favorite or have some sort of sentimental value to the child, even if you don't understand what that sentimental value is. This is their list that no matter what happens, and no matter who asks, they have full permission to say no. When they say no to one of the items on their list, you have to support their choice. This is where the other child is going to give you those big puppy eyes and likely tell that your child isn't sharing, if they're old enough to verbalize that. You've got to have your kid's back here and inform the other child that Johnny doesn't have to share his favorite shark toy, but there are other sharks he can play with.

Giving your child the support and the empowerment with making that decision on what toys they share and what toys they don't will not only have a more positive impact on their behavior, it may even have a positive impact on their relationship with you. Sometimes if the other child is crying, it's hard to ignore it, and fight the urge to make your child share something that you know they don't want to share. Don't stand for another mom trying to make your child share their favorite toy either. Now, I'm not telling you to throw down with Debora at the park. I'm just saying to use your voice and have your kid's back. Debora will just have to give you dirty looks from the pavilion. She's used to being wrong anyway. She doesn't like Starbucks. And who doesn't like Starbucks, but some fictional filler character to move a story along? Oh, yeah. That's Debora. Well, you get my point. Don't let other moms bully you into making your kid share their favorite things.

Does that mean that your kid shouldn't be bothered to share other things? No. Absolutely not. Children should be taught to share their things. Not only does it teach how to be altruistic to their fellow human being, but it can help teach them empathy. Empathy is something that even some adults struggle with. Being able to put yourself in someone else's shoes and understand how they might be feeling helps us relate to the world. Sharing is something that encourages self-reflection and opens the door to learning behaviors such as compromising. I love sitting back and watching children figure things out on their own. You can see their little brains working, and hear squeaky voices navigating the ins and outs of how to equally divide objects, or the amount of time each of them can have with a single object.

When I taught preschool, we worked a lot on sharing, and we encouraged problem solving skills. Parents have a tendency to want to solve things for their children. When we solve our children's problems for them when they're little, they won't learn how to work through problems on their own. Sitting back and allowing them to go through the problem-solving process can be empowering for them. It will help build their confidence. Sure, it's easier to just say, "here, let me do it." Do your best to refrain. They will figure it out. Only help if they have absolutely given it their very best effort. I like to stay nearby and encourage them to try. Sometimes that looks like me just saying encouraging words, and other times it looks like me modeling what it is they're trying to do, and then giving them the chance to do it themselves. Sometimes it's watching nervously while they figure out the jungle gym or standing nearby while they attempt to climb a tree. Other times it's telling three children that are fighting over one toy that they can figure it out and watching quietly while they do just that. It can be a wonderful experience, or it can be an upsetting experience, but it's their experience. No matter which way it goes, they learn from it.

Watching your child figure out the ways of the world can be nerve wracking. Especially, when we know we could fix it if we just swooped in. I want you to think about how you would feel if every time you tried to do something on your own, your boss or a coworker came in and did it for you, without ever asking. You would probably start getting annoyed pretty quickly, and you'd likely be pretty terrible at your job. You don't learn through osmosis. You learn through doing. Trying to figure out when to help and when to sit back can be tricky. You know, like the RUN DMC song. It's tricky, tricky, tricky, tricky. I can't tell you when the best time to step in is. Each child is different. They each have different tolerance levels. They each have different temperaments. They're each at different developmental stages. When you intervene will be based on so many things. You know your kid best. You know what it looks like when your kid is about to reach their breaking point. Step in before then. Trying to think straight when you're frustrated is difficult even for adults, so when you see that frustration building, maybe ask if they want help. If they decline, let them do it. If they don't, help them, but don't do it for them. Walk them through the steps, whether it's problem solving a sharing issue, or trying to zip and button their pants by themselves. Find a way that you can help them without completing the task for them.

Teaching independence comes up throughout their lives but encouraging them to try things on their own builds the confidence for them feel brave enough to try to do things on their own when they're older. Parenting is a balance between nurturing a child and raising an adult. You want to make sure you are giving a child as much love, warmth, and affection they can stand, but you also don't want to baby them because they are going to grow up and be shocked that the world doesn't hold them as a precious gem. I think some people think when others say the world isn't going to be kind to their kids, they are saying for parents to give them hard life lessons. I've noticed parents get very upset when someone says this phrase, or something similar. It's full on mama bear mode for some. They retort with something along the lines of, "the world is cruel enough, so I'll love on them while I can." Or "So, I should be mean to my kid to teach them life lessons because the world will?" No one is telling anyone to be mean to their kid. No one is saying stop loving on them. What people are saying is, you're raising adults, and coddling your kid, rushing to fix things, or springing into action to prevent them from experiencing their own consequences makes you feel like you're doing the right thing, but you're doing them a disservice in the long run.

At the typing of this book, my 11-year-old had a school project, and it's due today. It's 4:30 AM while I'm writing this, because I have 4 kids, and 4:30 is the only time I have quiet. So, this social studies project is extensive. He didn't tell me about it, nor did he bring me the information on it, so I had no earthly clue he even had a project until his teacher contacted me two days ago. As I stated before, I work full time. 2 days' notice on a weekday is not enough time to do all of the research required to type up an accurate report and complete a diorama.

Would it be nice for me to drop everything and fix his problem? I'm sure he would think it's great. I'm sure his teachers are expecting me to do that. I'm not. I'm in the 5th grade. This is not my project. I have talked to him about using his time at school to do his work on this project. Yeah, they've been giving them time in class to work on it. He hasn't been writing anything, and last night when I had solid time to help him, he was busy procrastinating, and trying to do anything else but the project. So, his project will be late.

I'll still help him get it done, but if he's not in a rush, I'm not in a rush. It's not my project, and his failure to inform me and plan, is not my emergency. This is something that adults don't even realize sometimes. Your failure to plan is not my emergency. Have you ever met someone like that? They wait until the last minute to do something and then request help with this big thing. You watch them rush you along to finish helping them to get to their deadline in time. You feel like it's your deadline because they're rushing you to get something done that they should've done a long time ago. It could be a boss, your spouse, a friend, or even your sister that does stuff like this to you. Someone else's failure to plan is not your emergency.

What is going to happen if my son's project is late? Will his world end? No. It won't. 3rd grade is when they start transitioning to children writing down their own assignments. Schools even have these handy dandy planners for each kid. It's in their budget or something, like they care about our children (gasp). By 4th grade they stop helping them write in these planners and expect them to copy the assignment off of the board, but they are reminded. In 5th grade, they are expected to know to copy the assignments off of the board, which are there at the beginning of class. The school no longer tells the parents what the assignments are, because they are preparing them for middle school. So, my sweet, silly, funny child had multiple opportunities to learn how to use his planner (he knows how, I've seen him use it for things he wants to do), and he had plenty of opportunities to write down this assignment or get another copy of the assignment to bring home. I'm not an ogre. I would have helped him, and we could've had a completed project to turn in this morning. Instead, he will be one of the few kids not turning in his project because he didn't give anyone enough notice to appropriately help him. This year has been a struggle with him academically, because he is just not motivated to do his work outside of school, so he doesn't bring it home. This is where those old natural and logical consequences come in.

He will likely lose a few points for turning his project in late, and it may make him feel badly. It'll be OK. He will get over it. Next time he has a project, he will bring the information home in a timely manner, or he will fail the assignment. So, while rescuing him would put me in a panic, but warm my mommy heart, I just can't because he will continue to think I'm going to fix things. The responsibility will shift back on to me, when at this age, his school assignments are completely on him, as they should be. While children are in need of our support, we shouldn't enable them from becoming full responsible human beings. Stepping in all the time to save your children anywhere from sharing to homework, can send them the signal that they are not capable of problem solving, and that you will always be there to fix it, so why even try.

19

Gendering Pitfalls & How to Avoid Them

Gendering is a hot topic lately, and truthfully, I didn't even think about putting this chapter in my book. If we are being truly transparent here, I got stuck, and what do I do when I'm stuck? I ask Facebook. I put out a call for things parents of little ones would like to learn about. It sat quiet for a little while, and then it exploded with all kinds of good topics that I had not previously considered to put in a book about behaviors. When my friend brought up gender labeling, I had a lightbulb moment. I know, cliché right? I'm not some 1800's scientist, but I had a lightbulb moment, nonetheless. Gender roles, and expectations can absolutely cause behavior problems. Some of us like to consider ourselves as so "woke" that we wouldn't do such a thing, while some of us are so "woke" that we need to take a nap. We've all met those people. They take a notion and pump it up by five hundred thousand. I'm all for allowing children to find what gender role they want to take on, and even encouraging them to buck the system of gender stereotyping as a whole. I'm not down for randomly assigning an X as the sex of your child on a birth certificate. I know, I'm probably going to get hate mail, and people will show up with their pitchforks and demand I be burned at the stake.

My issue with using X as a sex is that it's not entirely accurate. We are talking about sex, not gender. Gender is what you identify as. Sex is biological. Does that mean you can't be biologically male, but present and identify as a female? No. It means that you were born with male or female organs. Unless we are going to start running DNA on every baby born to see how many male, and female chromosomes they have to accurately give them the listing of X if they have XXY or and XYY pattern. There are whole studies on these different combinations of sexing chromosomes outside of our normal XX and XY. I feel like a lot of people mix up gender and sex. I could just be old school in that aspect, or maybe my biology teachers in high school and college sucked at explaining the difference to us. I don't know. This is strictly my view on it, and you can look up the articles yourself. I actually think researching this topic would help some parents accept their transgender children. To know that there are multiple combinations of sex chromosomes outside of the two we've been taught can be mind blowing, and also freeing. So, my point in this chapter is not to get into assigning the appropriate sex at birth, it's to talk about gender and how gender stereotypes and biases can shape our parenting.

Gender stereotypes are the roles each sex is supposed to play. If you were assigned female at birth, you're supposed to be feminine and soft, not too loudly spoken, and submissive. If you were assigned male at birth, you're supposed to be in charge, aggressive, successful, and strong. The list for these stereotypical characteristics could go on forever. I've only taken the liberty to list the first few that popped into my mind. Most people when they find out they're having a girl, they go out and buy everything pink and purple, with flowers and dainty little ladybugs on them. If they're having a boy, everything is blue and green, with trucks and things on them. It's not your fault. We are conditioned to do this. Everything in the media makes us believe this is the way it's supposed to be. This is what our parents did to us, and what their parents did to them. Although at some point the colors got switched. It used to be pink for boys and blue for girls. I don't remember the time frame. Maybe in the 30's. Don't quote me on that. I didn't learn that in school, or through my own research. I learned it from a Buzzfeed article, so take it with a grain of salt. Is this to say that dressing your child up in gender specific clothes is going to damage them? Yes. You're ruining your children with that Doc McStuffins shirt. I'm kidding. I hope you didn't drop the book and run after that last sentence.

You're not going to ruin their lives or create trolls just because you dress them in gender specific clothing or buy them gender specific toys. My suggestion to help combat this gender stereotype is to make sure that you are not only buying them gender specific clothing, unless they like it. If they like gender specific clothes buy the whole store out. If you have a girl that's a "tomboy" or prefers gender neutral, or male clothing, let them wear what they want. Let them wear what makes them feel comfortable. It is not going to be the end of the world if your little girl likes to wear jeans and t-shirts instead of big JoJo bows and sparkly things. Not all girls like that. Not all girls shop in the girls' section. Now, this is typically easier for parents of girls to handle. You don't really hear about parents forcing their girls to wear pretty dresses if that's not what the child prefers. You do, however, hear about, or even know someone who forces their boy to wear boy clothes, when they just want to wear that princess dress.

Children pay attention to your reactions. It may start with wanting to wear their sister's princess dress, and if you react negatively, they won't dare to be brave enough to tell you they want to wear that pink skirt to school. We cannot place our internal judgements on our children. Most of the time, preschoolers want to try on the other genders items. They like dressing up. They like pretending to be a boy or girl when they are the opposite. Does that mean they are transgender? Some of them may be, but most of them are not. They are simply doing what is developmentally appropriate and normal. They're trying on the baseball cap, just like they would try on mom's high heels, or work boots. They like to play dress up. They like to try on gender roles. Don't discourage it. In fact, you should probably just mind your grown folk business and not intervene at all. Observe and keep it moving. Unless you want to play with them and not mention one way or the other what you think about them cross dressing, you probably should just be quiet. We inadvertently place our world views on our children and then question why they don't tell us these big things later in life. We condition them not to when we react in a big, and negative way to something as small as child's play. Same goes for a big positive reaction. Children want to please their parent, so your reaction matters. It's better to not react at all to these gender specific things.

Gender stereotyping goes further than clothing, it also goes for toys. Mix up the selection of toys your kids have. Make sure you get your boys some dolls. Boys should have dolls, because boys become fathers, they become teachers, and nurses. Boys *are* caregivers. Don't make them feel like they should be ashamed for wanting to expand on their nurturing side. If boys play with baby dolls and learn how to hold them and care for them, maybe, just maybe they won't be terrified to hold an actual baby when they get older. Maybe not. Who knows, but it certainly wouldn't hurt. Throw in some trucks and action figures for your girls. The point is just to make sure they have a variety of toys, dress up clothes, and regular clothes to choose from. I'm not saying you have to go all out and buy multiple outfits that do not fit your child's gender. I'm only saying if you're in a store and they say "I want this shirt" when you're shopping for new clothes, get them that shirt. Don't limit them to what you think is gender appropriate. Let them explore the aisles of the of the other side and pick out whatever they want. They may look at you like you've just grown a new head, or they may look at you with excitement and look for the perfect toy or outfit for them.

Behavior issues can arise when we are forcing our gender specific ideas on our children. They may or may not act out aggressively, but they most likely will become depressed and anxious. They are just trying to express themselves, and your reaction, if it's negative can cause them to become confused and feel alone. The children at school will likely already make them feel confused and alone. You are supposed to be their safe place. Without support, they may become withdrawn. You may notice personality changes, like moodiness, or irritability. Maybe they're crying more easily, or you just notice they don't smile and laugh as much. Allowing them to venture to the other side of the aisle at the clothing or toy store, is just that. Checking out the other side. It's not encouraging or discouraging them. It's asking if they see anything they'd like to have on that side. It's opening the door to future conversations. It's letting them know that no matter what, I'm going to accept you.

Maybe mixing things up isn't for you. Maybe you think it will turn your child gay. I'm going to put your mind at ease. You can't catch "the gay." There is no scientific research finding that homosexuality is contagious. You can't turn someone gay. There is no evidence to suggest transgender people are contagious. Your child will not be turned one way or the other due to how you allow them to dress, or what toys you allow them to play with. If it did, there would be like 3 transgender people, and maybe 5 homosexual people, because most of the people that identify as LGBTQ were forced into their stereotypical gender roles, and they still turned out to be LGBTQ. It does not mean that they are not good people. It doesn't mean your child won't be a good person if they find that they are themselves a member of that community. It doesn't change who they are at their core. They're still your child. They still have the values that you've raised them with. And to be quite crude. I really don't understand why people are so concerned about what's going on in someone's pants, including their children's pants when they become adults. As parents when our children get a little older, we tend to hurt our own feelings. If they decide to trust you with the information about their sexuality, the problem typically isn't because they are LGBTQ. The problem is that our hopes and dreams, that they didn't ask for, and likely had no idea existed, were dashed, or changed. Guess whose problem that is? Not theirs. Guess who hurt your feelings and changed your life? You. Your child is just going about their business, living their best life and trying to become functional adults.

Our children's sexuality, or presumed sexuality really shouldn't even be a topic of discussion. Accepting that we are immersed in a society that places so much emphasis on gender roles is part of the solution. We have to accept it. Identify our own biases and do what we can to adjust them. When your little one is 0-5, you shouldn't be worried about their future gender identity or how they may or may not sexually identify based on their choice of dress up clothes, or toys. Their job at those ages is to explore, and play. Their job is to try on different roles to see how they fit while playing make believe. Most children will fall back into their assigned gender roles by first grade due to doing what they see. They will see at home "I'm a girl, and mom is too." They will model what they see. If it starts to become clear later that they may indeed have some gender identity questions, do your best to be unbiased. Love and support your child. Nourish their soul. Let them know they are not alone in this great big world that has already stacked the cards against them. Did you know that LGBTQ youth have a higher rate of suicide? Or that Black LGBTQ youth have an even higher rate still. When we had our children, we made a silent vow to ourselves to always protect them and love them. The harsh societal rejection and in many cases parental rejection, is killing our kids. Literally. LGBTQ or not, your child is *your* child, and you should protect them and love them accordingly.

How can you be supportive? When they are little, don't question their imaginative play with the opposite gender roles. Don't confine them to a box for their gender role. Don't force your child into a square hole, if they were beautifully made into a triangle. You didn't do anything to "turn them" anything other than a good human. Who they decide to settle down with in the future is their business. It does not affect your day to day life. If someone is rude or judgmental to you about their perceived notions on your CHILD...*those are not your people!* Find new people. Friends don't judge you, and they certainly don't judge your children. If it's your family giving you the side eye and gossiping. Love them from a distance. Your child needs you. Parental acceptance can make all the difference for an LGBTQ child. Do your best to create an environment where your child doesn't feel the need to "come out" to you. Create an environment where they can bring home a girl, boy, or dragon, and not feel the need to warn you about it first. Well, maybe they should warn you about the dragon if it has a tenancy to breathe fire or eat people. That's important. The point is, that we don't expect for our straight children to "come out" and make a grand, and terrifying announcement that they actually like the opposite sex. The thought of it probably makes you chuckle. We place way too much stock in kids' sex, and gender. The majority of children gay or straight are not having sex. Why are we so concerned about it? How about we just agree to make sure our kids become good humans?

I'm not sure if I covered all of the pitfalls on gender stereotypes. I kind of got off on a tangent, but it still fit within this chapter. If you're having difficulty accepting that you should accept your child, LGBTQ or not...just keep working on it. If you find that it's causing you distress, or a visceral reaction, talk to a therapist. Attend a local LGBTQ parent support group. Ask questions. Educate yourself on what it's like to live as an LGBTQ youth without parental acceptance. Educate yourself on the suicide rates of these youth. Once you have thoroughly educated yourself, and asked all of the questions, sit with your feelings for a while, and move on. Your child is their own person. They are not an extension of you, even if it feels like they are. Your child being gay, straight, or in between, has nothing to do with how they were raised. So, if you find that your son hates dressing as a boy, then don't force him to. Let him choose, and you keep being the fierce mama or papa bear that you are.

20

Confidence Booster

Confidence. How do we even build confident children? We touched on it some in another chapter, but we didn't really get into it well enough. Confidence is a learned behavior. Most children learn it at home, and creating confident children can help them academically, and socially. Confident kids aren't afraid to raise their hand in class, and they also aren't afraid to speak up for injustice. They aren't afraid to advocate for themselves or anyone else. Confident kids know who they are and make decisions accordingly. Parents don't typically set out to deplete their child's confidence. Some parents may, but they're mean. You're not. I can guarantee you that parents whose sole purpose in their children's lives is to tear them down, are not the ones buying this book. The parents buying this book, i.e., you are focused on doing your best to raise happy confident children. What are some ways to increase your child's confidence? I don't know. This is the end of the chapter.

Obviously, just kidding. Boosting confidence in kids really isn't rocket science. Be kind. Be supportive. Be encouraging. Set boundaries. Enforce consequences. Let them problem solve. Give appropriate compliments. See, super easy! Now, someone may be wondering what I mean by giving appropriate compliments, so I'm going to explain. Part of this goes back to the gender thing. A lot of parents tell their daughters how pretty, or beautiful they are without telling them how smart they are. This is not to say you can't ever tell your daughter she's beautiful. It's to say that her looks shouldn't be the focus on the majority of the compliments you give. Smart, leader, clever, persistent, helpful, these are all alternative compliments. We give these compliments sparingly to girls, and I'm not sure why. These sorts of compliments should be the bulk of the type of compliments you give, not just for girls, but for boys as well. Our language matters. If little girls only hear how beautiful they are, how will they ever know they're smart too? If we focus on how cute their outfit is, and how adorable they look in it, how does that encourage her to be a leader? Our words carry so much weight, and we have to pepper our girls with as much confidence as we give to our boys.

This isn't to imply that you shouldn't be pouring confidence into your boys as well, because you should. We just tend to push these types of compliments on boys without thinking about the ways we strip from their confidence. Have you ever told your son that boys don't cry? No, you haven't, because you wouldn't, but you know someone who does. Everyone knows someone who thinks that boys are somehow supposed to not express sadness or disappointment. Do you know what happens when we don't allow boys to express their sadness? They feel like something is wrong with them because they want to cry. They feel like when they are sad, the only acceptable expression is anger. So now you have a little boy who is acting out in a destructive manner, because he has been conditioned that he is only allowed to show anger or happiness. Boys, and men are full humans with a full range of emotions. We cannot stunt our boys' emotional growth, just because they're boys. I hate to be *that* author, but the whole "boys don't cry" thing is damaging. Come on, say it with me. Boys don't cry is damaging. You are telling them that there is something inherently wrong with them for having the natural inclination to cry. You are telling them that you, yourself, as a husband, father, uncle, brother do not cry, and therefore something must be wrong with them. You are damaging their psyche and their emotional growth and emotional intelligence. Boys cry. Men cry. They cry because they're human, and human being cry for a variety of reasons, sadness included.

So, the first real lesson in boosting confidence in children is to embrace and teach them to cope with their natural emotions. Emotions can be intense, and children having the proper tools to address their emotions helps them remain confident that they can do so when they are away from home. The second lesson would be to give appropriate compliments to your child. Tell them they're creative, good at science, or a great explorer. Focus on the things they're good at. Focus on how smart they are. For every appearance compliment you give, you should be able to give 5 nonappearance compliments. If you can't come up with 5 nonappearance compliments, then you need to take a step back and look for them.

Another one would be, accept them for who they are. They are individuals, and not your mini you, even if they physically look like they are. They are not you. They are not here to relive your life. They're here to live their own. Accept your children as they are. Your kid may be weird. Guess what? Weird is OK. Weird is fun, and colorful, and best of all, confident. If they have the confidence to be the weird kid, then you're doing pretty awesome. Believe it or not, the popular kid at school isn't always the most confident. In fact, they're usually pretty insecure due to feeling like they always have to fit into their role, which means they can't turn against societal norms. If you remember, there was a whole tween movie series around it. The star basketball player who wanted to do musicals and was feeling unsure and teased by his fellow students. You know what movies I'm talking about, even if you didn't have kids at that stage in life, you probably still knew the words to the songs of High School Musical.

Also, be involved. Go to their soccer games. Volunteer at school, if that's your jam. Communicate with their teachers regularly. Help them with homework. Ask them about their day, their friends, their likes and dislikes. Be involved. Show them that you care about what they're interested in. Show them that what they like matters. Show them that they are worth the effort of getting to know. They're not little roommates, they're children and need to know that their parents care enough to be involved in their lives. This does not mean hovering over them. It does not mean making all the decisions for them. It means stepping back and letting them come into their own personhood while you are involved enough to show you care about who they are becoming. It is so important to find the balance of saving our kids and allowing them to make their own mistakes as they figure out life. We all wish that they can avoid mistakes we made as we were growing up. Hopefully, they will, but if they don't, just be there for them. It breaks our hearts when our kids hurt, but we have to allow room for their own choices. The only thing we can do is give them the possible results of their choice, but in most cases, unless it's an absolute safety issue, we let them give it a try, and then a big hug and understanding words if things don't work out the way they hoped. This starts early. This is something you practice in late toddlerhood and preschool years. The stakes just get bigger as they get older, but by then you'll be a pro. Maybe not. Likely not. You'll just have different type of questions and different

Most likely, you don't even realize that the things you're doing with your toddler are confidence booster, or confidence breakers. We really don't think about it like that. If we did, we'd walk around too scared to say anything to our kids, for fear that we would break them in some way. The way you speak to your children, and the way you stop to listen to them when they speak, all helps build confidence. When you take the time to stop what you're doing for a few minutes to listen to whatever nonsensical story they're telling you, it's just another way to say to them, "you're important, and your words matter." Speaking kindly to them allows them to understand that they are deserving of respect. Confidence is born through kind words, effective discipline, respect, and supportive behaviors. What are supportive behaviors? Supportive behaviors are, allowing them to freely express themselves. It's knowing they like to act and finding a local playhouse that has an acting camp for preschoolers. It's seeing their good at soccer, and playing it with them in the yard, and being the loudest parent in the stands when they're playing on the field. It's respecting their personal boundaries. If they say they don't want to be tickled, then don't tickle them. If they say they don't want to hug a relative, don't make them. Obviously if they're talking about not wanting to eat food for three days while they eat their weight in Little Debbie cakes, you'd say no. What I'm talking about is their personal space boundaries.

Don't kill their curiosity. Children are natural born scientists, they love to explore and create. Children learn best through play, and not through someone lecturing them on how to do something. I always do an internal cringe when one of my friends tell me about a daycare their child is attending that has an extensive curriculum. They get homework, and learn how to write their names, letters and numbers. On the surface, it may seem that this daycare center is doing fantastic work at preparing children to enter elementary school.

In reality, daycare centers that boast intensive curriculums like these are not only developmentally inappropriate, but they may be causing undue stress and frustration on your child. Children are not designed to sit still for long periods of time. Their brains are not wired to diligently hold pencils the right way and copy letters from a piece of paper. Children learn through play. You want a daycare center that teaches your child the alphabet, great! Make sure they are teaching it age appropriately, through songs, dance, and having things labeled in the classroom. You want your kid to learn how to recognize their name, and even write it before they enter kindergarten? Fabulous, put their name on everything that's theirs. The more they see their name, the more they will recognize it. Letting them have blank pieces of paper and allowing them to try to copy their name is fine, *if* that's what *they* want to do.

We get so caught up in trying to make sure our children are the best, and the fastest at getting an education, we could be damaging them developmentally. They are not built for school. They're not build for traditional academics. They are built for play. They are built for exploration and crude child scientist experiments. What will happen if I put too much toilet paper in the toilet? Or I wonder what sidewalk chalk tastes like? They experiment, and usually we get annoyed, because, dude, sidewalk chalk is gross, don't eat that, but it's important to remember that they are learning. Learning the way that they were made to learn.

Remember back in the eighties and nineties how we used to learn? Kindergarten was just an extension of preschool. You didn't have to know Einstein's theory of relativity. In order to go to kindergarten in those days, we had to be able to recognize simple household items and animals, like an umbrella or a cat. We didn't have to already know how to count to 50, nor did we have to know how to write anything. We were at school to learn the basics of socialization, sharing and our ABC's. We weren't made to sit still for a developmentally inappropriate time. We weren't expected to be quite most of the day with very little time for free play to get out our excess energy. A lot of preschools are set up like 1st grade should be, and it's not fair to our kids, so if you have a little one that you send to preschool, or daycare, make sure they have a truly developmentally and age appropriate curriculum. If you're teaching them at home, don't stress out about making sure they have mastered everything. Just play with them and help them explore. Go on a bug hunt in your backyard. Blow bubbles and count how many seconds it takes for them to pop. Fingerprint out of vanilla yogurt with food coloring mixed in and let them lick it off of their fingers. It's OK if you lick it off of your fingers too, I won't tell.

Put your phone down. I mean, not right now if you're using it to read this book, but for sure if it's been a little while since you've seen your child's face without looking around your device. This one is hard, even for me. I'm on my phone way more than I'd like to admit to myself, and I know I need to do better. I remember when my older children were much younger, I didn't have this issue. We didn't have phones that are literally like little computers in our pockets. When my daughter was born, I didn't even have a cell phone. By the time my second child was born, I had a flip phone. A pink Motorola Razr. I thought that was the best phone ever. The screen even had what was supposed to be color. By the time my third child was born, I had a Blackberry, and I noticed I was more attached to it than I was to my previous phones, but still not to the extent that I'm attached to my iPhone. I have turned my car around from going to the store, just because I forgot my phone. I wasn't going to be gone more than 30 minutes. I would have survived.

Now that I have the youngest child, I have to make sure I take time to look at his face. Talk to him and give him the same attention I gave his siblings, because *he is more important than my phone.* I want him to know that I care about what he has to show me. Even though he can't talk, he still shows me things. He still checks to see if I'm watching when he busts a move in front of his house that plays music. He likes to make sure I see him when he finds something funny. Sometimes I miss it, if I'm working on the computer or phone, which I have to do if we want things like food and shelter, but I know he needs me to see him. So, if it's been a few minutes since I've seen him without a screen in front of my face, I will close everything and play with him. We parents also have a device addiction, and I'm the first to raise my hand saying I have one, but our kids see us with these light up boxes in front of our faces. They need to see us just seeing them. Showing them that they matter more than whatever article we are reading, or whatever Lisa just said on Facebook. We need to see them.

21
I Am Me, and You are You

I promise you that I wrote down the title of this chapter and could not remember for the life of me what it was supposed to be about. I just kept thinking this title makes no sense whatsoever. Why did I write this? Then I remembered. It's about individuality. We already learned how children are copycats, so how do we make sure they become individuals? That's the million-dollar question. The reality of it is, children are copycats, but they are also uniquely themselves. They are copying our behaviors and social norms, but they are not copying everything. Encouraging the things, they are showing interest in is one way to facilitate individuality. Maybe they just love cowboy boots, no matter what they're wearing. Let them wear them. Yes, even if it's 102 degrees outside and you know their feet will sweat. Maybe they have a hobby of wearing a different Halloween outfit every day. Give them a high five, because that's pretty awesome! Who would want to be a person, when you could be a tiger, or a dinosaur?

Individuality is expressed in so many different ways, and as long as we are encouraging their individuality, then we are sowing seeds of confidence. I remember when my second son was 2-6, it was a long phase...he was Iron Man. He had every Iron Man costume imaginable, but when he wasn't wearing one, he introduced himself as Iron Man. In fact, on his very first day of 2-year-old preschool, his teacher asked what his name was, and he makes the deepest, raspiest voice his little two year old self could muster, and says "I'm Iron Man," with his little fist balled up at his side. He immediately smiled and we all busted out laughing, because, who knew he was going to say that? I will let you know that I did not name my child Iron Man. I'm not even sure he saw the movie at that point, but he did have the action figures and costume. It was a very interesting period of time. I thought he was going to stay Iron Man forever, and I'd have to legally change his name to fit his identity. Thankfully, by the time he entered 4th grade, he was no longer interested in dressing up as Iron Man for Halloween, but even if he were, I'd let him. It's part of his individuality.

Expressing your individuality is not always easy, especially once kids reach grade school. In preschool, kids are still pretty mellow about others doing things they like without judgement. Once they get into upper elementary school, the gloves start to come off, so our job is to build self-confident children before they find themselves defending who they are to their peers. Peer pressure to conform can be difficult to weather, even for adults. So, making sure that we are creating an environment where are children can safely express themselves when they are younger is vital to having the confidence to face down bullies when they're older. Let them learn to be comfortable in who they are when they're little. Continue to give them words of affirmation as they get older. Sometimes this means biting our tongue, even when we think they look ridiculous. This means listening to their opinions on things that are different than yours, even if you think they aren't old enough to have an opinion at all.

Though our children are not our friends, we are their first friends. We teach them how people are supposed to treat each other, so our words to them really matter. The things we say about others in our children's ear shot matters. You may be saying "that orange is gawd awful on Rebecca," and didn't realize that your little one has developed a fondness for the color. Does that mean you think all orange is awful? No. It just means you thought it didn't do Rebecca any justice, but your child doesn't know that. All they heard was orange was awful. It probably won't scar them for life or anything, but it may alter the way to talk about the color orange. This goes for any situation really. If it's something that isn't for a child's ears, try your best not to say it in front of your child. Not just because they may change their favorite color from orange to blue, but because you can bet your sweet tail, they're going to tell Rebecca what you said. Why? Because kids like to embarrass us. I think it's accidentally on purpose, but they'll never tell us why they like to embarrass us.

Speaking of embarrassing. There was a time that my middle son was younger, and we went to Target, a moms mini vacation spot. Well, he wasn't old enough to be left to his own devices while I went to the bathroom, but he was old enough to talk and know that I was going potty. The bathroom at Target wasn't full, but there was someone in the stall next to us. I proceed to go to the bathroom, and my sweet, sweet, three-year-old says loudly "Mommy, can I pull that string hanging out?" The woman next to us laughed so hard, I thought she was going to fall off the toilet. Kids, man. They just love to say and do random things that will make you turn five shades of red. So, you better believe if you say something about someone else in front of your little one, they're going to tell it. Even if you didn't say anything terrible, they will still say something terribly embarrassing. Like when my sister was little, she saw a woman in the drug store with a mole on her nose. She yells as the lady is going by "that lady has a witch nose!" The woman was probably just as mortified as my mother. My sister was maybe, five. She didn't really know any better.

I'm so easily distracted when talking about kids and the random things they say. Getting back on track, expressing individuality within painting, dress up, or even entertainment is something that should continue to be encouraged as they get older. My daughter has a friend who loves makeup. He loves to dress in drag for school events, but you know what he loves most? Being accepted at school and at home for who he is. I heard his mother talking to him as he was getting ready to come ride with us somewhere. She didn't mention that he shouldn't be wearing makeup. She told him that his liner was uneven on one side, and that he needed a different shirt on because he didn't match. And that was only because he asked. She supports him being him. He's fabulous and we want him to continue to be fabulous for as long as he wants to. It takes a brave person to turn gender norms upside down, especially in the deep south, but there he is, living his best life, and his mom and grandparents support him all the way.

I can't say how he was raised. I can't say how long it took for his mother and grandparents to come around, or if they've always been in his corner. But I can say that he continues to thrive in the environment that he's being raised in. This is what we want for our own children. We want them to be able to be true to who they are as individuals. I can't say that your son would be interested in wearing makeup, but if he's interested in baseball, or dance, support and nurture his individuality either way. If your daughter is into hockey, or cheer, show up and show out at her games or events. Our kids depend on us to tell them that who they are is OK. Who they are is good enough. Who they are is worthy of love, praise and acceptance. That's what our kids are craving when they begin to express themselves as individuals. They don't need us to put doubt in their heads. Believe me, there will be plenty of people along the way that are going to question who they are as individuals. Their parents shouldn't be one of them.

22

Quality Time vs Quantity Time

I've been around a lot of parents, mostly women, because let's be real, women hold this world up. I've helped a lot of families who were struggling with their children's behaviors, and time is something that I've noticed can go one of two ways. I've worked with stay at home moms, who spent practically every waking moment with their children, and their children behaved in a manner that I could only call atrocious. I don't like to describe a child's behavior as something that is that terrible, but they literally behaved like some caged zoo animals that were just allowed out into an open space for the first time. These poor mamas looked the part of a frazzled beast tamer, as well. They looked exhausted, and overwhelmed. Their voices sounded as if they would breakdown crying if I asked the wrong question. These poor mamas were defeated, and all I wanted to do was hug them, and tell them that they were doing the best they could.

When I would spend the hour observing these families, one thing became very clear. Their children were being ushered from one project to the next. Not given a chance to get bored or be from underneath their mother's. I'm not sure if this is because the moms were afraid the children would inevitably burn the house down if they were supervised like a mouse by a hawk waiting to swoop in for their morning breakfast, or if it was because somewhere down the line, these mamas' information got crossed. Did someone tell them they needed to play with their children with scheduled activities every minute of the day? Did someone tell them that? If someone has fed you this lie, or you're trying to keep up with Kimberly on Facebook, just stop. I know Kim, yes, this is a real friend. She's in a different league than us. We all just sit back and watch her in awe. But let me tell you something about Kim, she is not planning out her children's activities for the whole day. She's not. She does big projects with them for special occasions. She shuttles her kids to activities, but she also lets the get bored. She leaves them to their own devices. Her children do not have a lack of imagination.

Kim spends a lot of time with her children, partly because her daughter is in competition cheerleading (hi Abbie!), but I promise, her children have lives outside of her, as they should. So, when you see her, or someone like her uploading fantastic crafts on Instagram, know that there's a difference between quality time, and quantity time. These moms that I mentioned about are spending oodles and oodles of time with their children, and it's burning them out. There children aren't benefiting from it either. Yes, their mom is there, but is she mentally there? Is she emotionally able to handle spending 8 in your face hours with her kids while ushering them from one activity to the next within her own home? Are these children learning how to be independent, or are they learning how to push mama's buttons? News flash, y'all. It's usually the latter. Children are great button pushers, but just like you, they need space. They need space to play and explore. Getting in trouble for things they shouldn't be doing, like seeing if they can turn their little sister into a mummy with the bulk toilet paper you just got at Sam's or Costco. Obviously, we would stop them, but that's how memories are made. That's how kids learn cause and effect. We've already removed the safety hazards from their reach, so why can't they spend some time playing alone while you work on something you need to get done?

I don't mean plopping them on an iPad or phone, so you can load the dishwasher without them destroying the house. If you're feeling personally attacked right now, that must mean I'm talking to you. I'm sorry. I'm not attacking you. I'm just telling you what I've observed while working with families and being paid a pretty terrible salary to address these children's behaviors. Through my work, it was very interesting. These children were diagnosed with all kinds of mental health issues, but mostly ODD, which is what they call Oppositional Defiant Disorder. This diagnosis basically meant that the children didn't listen and had a difficult time following direction.

Typically, when I worked with these children, they didn't have some sort of disorder. They had poor boundaries at home, and very inconsistent consequence with parents like continually saved them from natural consequences when they happened. Sometimes, these were children that had stay at home mothers that spent an ungodly amount of time with them. At times, these poor moms were getting cussed out, while the mother said in a soft voice "don't speak to me like that." Look, now, me and little Nicholas are about to have a come to Jesus meeting if he doesn't start speaking to his mother like he has some sense (I would say in my head). Out loud I would say," give him some space. I'll talk to you for a few minutes until he can calm down."

You know, the key to many of the behavior issues in these homes were space. The children needed to feel like they could exist without someone hovering over them to make sure they were existing properly. I've witnessed a child throw things at her mother, because her mother would follow her from room to room. I would continue to say, "give her space," and the mom would continue to follow her child from room to room arguing back with her. Then when things started flying, mom started screaming, but still following her child. "I can't help you, if you aren't going to listen." I'd say as calmly as possible. Eventually, mom listened and came to vent to me about how her child behaves. About 20 minutes later, the child emerges, apologizes on her own and then goes back to her room. Her mom promptly follows. The cycle started all over again. The issue was, the mom felt like she needed to spend an exorbitant amount of time with her daughter because she worked full time and had a part time job as a coach. But this part time job, also brought her daughter along to be coached within her mother's eyesight. This mother worked at the sister school for her daughter's school, so her child never felt like she could be herself without overseers reporting back. This is a lot of time to spend together.

This isn't to say that you shouldn't spend time with your children, because, obviously you should. You just shouldn't smother them with the you can't function without me making sure that you're still breathing kind of attention. This is to say that just because you spend an abundant amount to time with your children doesn't mean you're spending quality time with them. Quality time is the time you spend with your child really seeing them. Slowing down long enough to notice those natural pale blonde streaks in their hair from the sun. Paying attention to know that they really don't like butter pecan ice cream, because the pecans are piling up on one side of the bowl. Quality time is understanding that you can't be with them every waking moment of the day, so you're making the most of the time you have with them.

You can spend quantity time with your children without ever breaching the *quality* time perimeter. So, before we move on, let's go ahead and dispel the notion that you're supposed to spend all your waking time fawning over your children. Let's not pretend that you're a bad parent because you allow them to spend some time in their room (gasp) alone. If you've been killing yourself trying to meet this very unrealistic and unnecessary image, I'm giving you permission to stop. If you're beating yourself up because you aren't spending enough time with your kids because you're a single mom right now, and you have to work two jobs to make ends meet. I'm giving you permission to stop. Stop beating yourself up. Stop comparing yourself to other moms on social media, because let me tell you a secret. Their poop stinks too!

They have their own problems that they just aren't posting about. I mean, who would post about all of the horrible no good awful stuff they had going on for the world to see? No one. Even the mommy bloggers that seem to be sharing the "real" side of parenting. They're not telling you the whole story. They're not telling you that their husband is having an affair and they don't know what to do. They're not telling you their kid called them the B word and then threw a shoe at their head. They're not telling you most of the things that are going on in their lives. They're telling you just enough to stay relatable, and keep you coming back for more of their videos and blog posts. This doesn't make them liars. It doesn't even make them deceitful. It makes them human, and it keeps the boundary of personal life and public life, because, as much as we may love them, they are not our friends. I know, it's sad. I feel like they're my friends too, but they aren't. They have their own lives, and their own real-life friends. They allow you to see a glimpse into their lives, but they aren't obligated to share everything with you.

This goes for those friends you knew in high school too or haven't seen in several years. They aren't sharing everything on social media, and they aren't required to tell you everything. Even though we may know them, we aren't in their inner circle. Do you share everything going on in your home on social media? You don't. For the same reasons no one else does. So, take the focus off of quantity, and replace it with quality. If you spend a lot of quality time with your child, that's great if they're enjoying it as much as you are, but if you're spending an excessive quantity of time with your children, and it doesn't seem like any of you are enjoying it then stop. Yes, stop spending so much time with them. Still supervise them from a distance but let them figure things out. Let them get into things. Did you know that letting children climb, play, and essentially get themselves into situations through play that they have to get themselves out of increases problem solving skills? Guess where they need problem solving skills? In math, social studies, and science class. They also need it in life. Guess who has trouble solving problems right now, Generation Z. Not because of anything they did, they were just raised differently. They were the generation that had internet from the time they were born. They were also the generation who were mostly parented through helicopter parenting. These kids still need their parents to call the college to figure things out for them. My daughter is part of this generation, and I swear she was on the border of a panic attack when I made her straighten out her mess with the college herself. She also signed heavily when I told her I wasn't scheduling her appointments.

Sitting and helping side by side is not the same as doing it for them. Sitting there while they figure it out and you back them up is learning. Putting them in a position where they never have to do anything on their own because their parent has always jumped in to rescue them protects them from the harsh realities of their decisions, but it doesn't prepare them to function in the world. While rescuing your child protects your heart and their own, it does nothing for their future self. Not all Generation Z was raised with helicopter parents, some were raised like my daughter, and aren't at all shocked when they have to figure out adulting on their own, but just like a new driver, when an experienced driver is in the car they are going to look to them for guidance. Guide when needed, but don't do it for them. Don't rescue them from everything. Let them experience natural and logical consequences. Let them get themselves out of a situation. That means if you told your little one not to climb and they did it anyway, you stand under them to catch them if needed, but you let them figure out how to get down, just like they figured out how to get up.

Spending quality time with your children will look like 15 minutes before bed some days. While other times, quality time will look like taking your middle child on an only child day to do all the things they want to do. Quality time often happens in the in between times. Snuggle time before bed or baking cookies on a Saturday morning. Quality time isn't usually an all-day event. It's times in the day that show your children that they are seen and heard. That their opinions matter. It shows them that you trust them to spend time alone, so when you spend time together you have the patience to love on them positively. It also provides them with a parent that isn't going through the motions because they have to. It teaches them how to play by themselves and use their imaginations.

Take a moment and think about the time you spend with your children. Do you spend most of it wishing it were nap time? Do you spend most of the day wishing it were an acceptable time to open that bottle of wine you've been saving? I challenge you to really think about the amount and type of time you spend with your children and see if there's any room for you to make changes. If you feel like you need to adjust in one place or another, make the adjustments. If you think you got this, and don't need to change anything in this area, then that's great!

23
Don't Laugh at That

Children are funny, like hilariously funny! I'm not sure why they're so funny, because most of the time they're not even trying. Maybe it's because they are still so new here, and figuring things out, which can be side busting at times. Maybe it's because they're going to be the next great comedian. Who know. All I know, is children are funny and I hope they never stop being so silly. For example, my one year old thinks it's hilarious to scare people. He's not really scaring anyone, but he thinks he is, and just his little belly laughs cause us all to crack up with him. He has taken to "scaring" one of our cats. Not all of them, just one, because she indulges in his nonsense and runs away when he does his little jump and fake scream. The cat that runs away is not afraid of the baby. I don't want PETA coming after me for animal cruelty. She likes to play with him, and sees he thinks it's funny when she runs, that's it. Nothing else to see here.

When my middle son was younger, he couldn't say the blended "st" sound, so things got... interesting sometimes. His "st" sounds came out sounding like the "d" sound, and he loved to find sticks to play with. I'll let you use your imagination on what he actually called them. We would literally have to turn our heads to keep from laughing when he said it. Why? Because when kids know you think something is funny, they just keep doing it over and over. The last thing we wanted was for him to be walking around at church or wherever yelling out stick, which sounded like a dirty word for a male appendage. That's the thing with kids. You can't laugh at a bad behavior even once, or it will stick. They'll keep doing the thing you laughed at, just trying to get that same reaction. When it doesn't get them the laugh they hoped for, they are confused, but will keep trying.

This is where we as parents become embarrassed, and sometimes frustrated, due to our children's behaviors or potty mouths, not really connecting the dots that they were following our cue. It's especially embarrassing when they exhibit these behaviors in front of visitors, or out in public. A lot of times, parents will laugh off this behavior, once again sending the message that this is amusing. Other times, parents become embarrassed, and may react more harshly than they would have on any other occasion. This is confusing to the child and will likely hurt their feelings. I'm not sure which situation is worse for the parent and child, but I do know it can't feel great for either of those scenarios to play out. The things little ones say and do can be shocking sometimes, but we are the models they are continually looking to for examples of appropriate behaviors. Remember when I said, children want nothing more than to please their parent? It really is true. Though at times it may seem that they are doing everything in their power to make sure your hair falls out prematurely or turns gray like Storm from X-Men, they really just want you to be happy with them. This is why laughing or smiling when they exhibit unacceptable behavior causes a repeat of that behavior.

Then again, there are some parents that allow their children to cuss, because they don't want to alter their own language to model appropriate language to their child. I'm not saying there's anything wrong with this. I...I just have...questions? If we are allowing children to use sentence enhancers when they are two and three, are we also teaching them that others may not be accepting of their language. Are we only allowing them to talk like this at home? Does this cause some sort of mixed message or identity confusion? Does this make them feel like they are the adult? And my last question; what exactly are they getting from using inappropriate language? I don't know the answers to these questions, because we didn't study it, and I've never run across it in my professional life. I've heard it in the store. "Sharon, you're p*ssing me off" is something I heard a kid say from the cart at Walmart. Yeah, Sharon was his mom. No, she did not correct his language. She gave it to him right back.

I'm not going to pretend to understand their relationship. Maybe she wasn't his mom. Maybe she was his much older sister who was stuck babysitting him. Maybe it was none of my business, which is the way I treated it. There's just something that catches you off guard when you hear a young child swearing at an adult. Especially an adult that's their parent. I'm sure I'm not the only person that blushes and wonders what in the whole wide world of Jesus is going on when you hear a small child swearing like they pay bills. To be sure it's not only me. I grew up in a house where we weren't allowed to say butt, fart or lie, because they were all cuss words in my mom's eyes. We also couldn't say pee, the "t" word for breasts, or panties. Actually, I still can't say the last two. It gives me a weird shiver just to even type it (does a full body shake). Now that I got that off of my chest, you guys can probably see why I'm reaching for my pearls when I hear a sweet baby child swearing.

I promise you, it must be a southern thing, because my family is probably the most southern northerners you'd ever meet. It kind of makes sense though. My grandmother was from Tennessee, and my grandfather was from Alabama. My grandmother didn't allow us to say those things either, which means she definitely didn't allow my mom or her fifty (actually 8) siblings to say it either. This is probably also the reason that my mother, at the ripe age of (none of your business because I'm not too old for her to "pop"), still doesn't say them. It may seem silly to some, that a grown woman of an undisclosed age doesn't even say butt, because she finds it offensive, but everyone is raised differently, and these things stick.

How do you handle when your kid does something funny, but super inappropriate? My go to is to turn around until I have regained control over my face. Sometimes, I have to excuse myself. There was something that happened, I don't remember what because I must be going senile at the ripe age of 38. It's likely baby brain, but here we are, not remembering something that almost made me pee my pants. Anyway, it was when my big boys were little, and my middle son said or did something that caused me to literally leave the house. I mean, I just looked at him and immediately walked outside and around the back of the house. Cracked up laughing until I had actual tears rolling down my face. I got myself together long enough to go back and correct the behavior. He was none the wiser. My oldest son asked if we had any mail. He just assumed because I went outside, I went to go check the mail. Sweet boy. I just could not laugh in front of them. I knew that it would be a colossal mistake, especially with my middle son. He is like the class clown of the house. Everything is funny. Everything is silly. Everything is just extra with him. It shouldn't be a surprise that he wants to be an actor.

When your kids are silly, there's an endless supply of things going on in everyday life that you can find to be silly about with them. If they are just your average kids that get tickled at potty jokes, tell them some potty jokes. At this age, they love "dad jokes." I don't know what it is about "dad jokes," but kids think they are hilarious. Let your kid tell you jokes as well. I should warn you though, you'll be there for about four hours waiting for them to get through one knock knock joke, but their silly little giggle will make up for the lost hours of your life. Whatever it is that you do, find fun and creative ways to make sure your kid gets the laughs they need. Belly laughs are the best, even for adults.

24
Daddy's House is More Fun

Oh, co-parenting. I don't know if I could ever say enough things on this topic. I co-parent. I co-parent with my ex-husband, and with my current husband. Why do I co-parent with both? Because if you have a child with someone, whether you're living together or not, you, my friend are co-parenting. Or at least doing some version of co-parenting. Most people don't think of co-parenting as something you do with your current spouse, but it absolutely is. So, stick around for this whole chapter, because I think everyone who has children could benefit from the information in this chapter. I don't know if you're going to want to grab a pen and write some of this down, but I don't think it would hurt.

The first thing you want to do when you're co-parenting with another adult is communicate. I don't care who you are co-parenting with. It could be a spouse, a grandmother, a sister wife, I really don't care, the number one way to success will be communication. Now, I saw this meme or whatever you want to call it on the interwebs saying that it's not about communication, it's about comprehension. If you are communicating effectively then you both should be comprehending. When you communicate effectively you are using I statements, as well as reflecting back what you heard and understood. This cuts down on confusion. Here's an example of both. "I really feel alone and frustrated when I have to make all of the appointments and get them there." Well the listening party may say something like "I'm super busy and don't have time." But if you disarm them with the I statement, where you're not accusing them of anything, you're simply stating how you are feeling, they will likely start trying to help you solve the problem. I mean, they could be a jerk about it and say too bad, but most people will try to help you figure out a way to not feel frustrated. You could close the sentence with "it would be super helpful if you could alternate appointment days with me. Is this something that you can do?"

Using the example in the last paragraph, let's take a look at a reflective statement. The issue is still the same, one parent needs help with appointments. Maybe they weren't as nice when they said what they needed. Maybe it sounded like this. "I'm doing all of the work by myself. I have to schedule and take them to all of their appointments while you're just sitting them playing with your little girlfriend. What is she, like 12!?" In this instance, the person listing to the rant would use a reflective statement and ignore the noise no matter how frustrated they may be. The reflective statement would sound like this. "It sounds like you're frustrated with me because I'm not helping as much as I could be with appointments. I'm sorry. If you need my help with getting them to and from appointments, I'd be happy to make arrangements." This is letting them know that you heard what they were asking and you're offering a solution.

This little change in communication can cut down on conflict between parents. We only see things from how they are affecting us.

If we are upset, we have a tenancy not accurately see things from the other person's point of view. This especially goes for someone that we feel like has caused us emotional pain in the past. You've likely worked hard to get past the anger and sadness felt that likely came with the end of that relationship, so you're more sensitive to their words and actions. If you are still married, then this serves the same purpose. It allows the tensions to come down to a more manageable level, so you can actually hear and understand what the other person is saying. Sometimes it means having to allow the person to vent before trying to reflect and correct an issue.

You can't correct an issue if someone is screaming at you. Let them get their frustration out, so long as they are not being abusive. Let them fuss, and scream while you sit there and listen, waiting for them to stop. While you're listening, be sure to actually listen. You are listening for ways you can help them. You are listening for a solution to offer them that is within your control. This may mean changing something that you're doing. I know, you're perfect, and they're the problem, but let's just indulge them and see what happens. This does not mean offer them a solution with an attitude. Yeah, you may be offering a solution, but your tone of voice may be calling them a female dog. Listen. When you have figured out what the problem is, and how you can fix it, count slowly to ten in your head before you speak if you find that you're upset.

Some of you may think I have lost my mind. You may be thinking I'm just a crazy pants therapist lady telling you to do things that aren't realistic. I'm not. I'm really telling you what works to open up the lines of effective communication and keep them open. This is obviously not for those of you that have abusive ex-partners. If you have an abusive ex-partner that you have to co-parent with, this strategy may work, but the boundaries have to be clear. Remember when I said you don't have to listen if they're being abusive? I know you do, it was literally like five seconds ago. This is super important when you have to speak with an abusive ex about your child.

You are not there to listen to them be abusive to you. In fact, you're not there to listen to anyone be abusive to you, ever. If someone starts name calling, you give them one warning. Tell them that you cannot continue the conversation if they are going to speak to you in that way. If they do it again, then end the conversation. If they are or were physically abusive to you in the past, please seek professional counseling to learn how to co-parent with your abuser if you have to do so. I would suggest an in between person and having an iron-clad custody agreement filed through the courts.

Co-parenting with someone that is toxic could be a whole book on its own, and actually, I believe there are books on this. One is called *Co-Parenting with a Toxic Ex: What to Do When Your Ex-Spouse Tries to Turn the Kids Against You* by Amy J. L. Baker and Paul R. Fine. There's another book named *Joint Custody with a Jerk* by Julie A. Ross and Judy Corcoran. I have not read either of these books, so I'm not sure how good they, are, but they will definitely give you more information than this chapter will about co-parenting with an abusive personality type.

Tip number two, did I give these names or just start naming the tips? I don't know, so we are just going to go with it. Tip number two for co-parenting successfully compromising. When you're trying to co-parent, you have to be flexible. Acting like a rigid ogre doesn't really help anyone and doesn't make people want to co-parent with you. Yes, there should be some sort of rules and order in place for visitation for you to follow, but if a weekend needs to be switched or afternoon pick up has be changed, then we should try to be understanding as fellow human being. You don't have to bend until you break but bending should absolutely be an option for both parties. Children benefit from seeing their parents get along well. Not only are you teaching them that two people who are no longer together, can and do get along, you are also modeling good problem-solving skills.

Good co-parenting isn't just for those that are divorced, or "broken up." Two people can be happily married, and not co-parent well together, and if you can't co-parent well together when you're married, you certainly won't be able to co-parent well together if you ever seek divorce. I find it interesting that when people think of co-parenting, they always think of it within the context of broken families, and not families that are still intact. Not co-parenting well as an intact couple, can actually cause issues in your relationship, as one parent may feel like they are shouldering the majority of the parental role, while the other is not consistently holding up their end. These feelings can cause resentment, which can seep out as snippy remarks, or irritability that results in shouting matches. When the main parent complains, the other may adjust their behavior for a while, but eventually they slip back into their roles and the resentment starts to build all over again. This is such a difficult situation, because you want to be able to feel like you're sharing the parental responsibilities with your partner, and if you're not, it's usually up to the already overburdened parent to speak up to enact change.

Truth be told, if I know someone else is going to do the bulk of the work, then why would I bust my tail to help when I don't have to. The bulk of the parenting assignments generally fall on the shoulders of the female, and women are so very conditioned to feel guilty if they can't do all the things, all of the time, that they very rarely ask for help. And if women do ask for help, it is most likely when they are at their boiling point or have already blown up several times. Ladies stop feeling guilty for asking for help. Just stop. Yeah...I know, it's not that simple. So, what I want you to do is ask for help anyway and sit in the feeling of uncomfortableness. It will pass, and eventually it will get easier to ask for help. Go back and reread Mommy Needs a Mimosa, I'll wait. Did you read it? That chapter also talks about asking for help and sharing the load.

So, the two things we talked about for successful co-parenting so far, is communication, and compromise. You also want to make sure you're not keeping score. A lot of people do this, and truthfully, it's damaging. The last thing someone wants to hear is all the times they didn't help out, or didn't follow through with something, especially if it wasn't something that happened all the time. Someone is much less likely to help you if you start the request with "I'm always doing everything, so you take him." Well no, if you're *always* doing everything then keep doing everything, is what they are likely thinking. This is a sure-fire way to get someone to stop listening to what you're saying, because they feel attacked, and like you're calling them a bad parent. And I don't know if you know this about parents, but they could be the worst parents in the world, but they will immediately get offended if they feel like someone is calling them a bad parent. Keep this in mind when speaking to your parenting partner.

I really could go on for another few chapters on this subject, but as I won't because I have so much more to cover, and very little time. This particular paragraph is for the inactive parent. You see the other parent struggling. There may be situations where you think to yourself, "I'm glad that's them and not me," or "I could never handle that." Yeah...those times. Those are the times that the other parent needs your help. They should not have to struggle through that situation on their own. These are your children too. If you know your children have teeth, ask your wife when was the last time they went to the dentist, and if she wants you to schedule an appointment *and* take them. Ask if they're due for physicals, or if it's their week to bring snack for preschool, or soccer. These are your kids. You know what they need, even if it's something that the other parent usually handles. They will welcome the help, I promise. Here's another tip, if they send you to the store to pick something up, take a picture of whatever it is they asked you to replace before you leave the house, so you don't have to call and have them walk you through the aisle. That is still taxing on their already over used mental capacity. I absolutely believe in your ability to be a great parent and partner.

Showing appreciation when one parent does something that you either couldn't do, or just really didn't want to do, and even showing appreciation for the assistance you get raising a child in general. Believe me, your partner, or ex-partner could probably be doing a whole lot less. It's also a proven fact, (it may not be, but in my head, it is) that when someone feels appreciated, they tend to want to do more. Humans thrive off of praise.

We're a lot like our four-legged barking friends in that way. Except, we don't want a milk bone. We want a thank you, or if you're at work, a raise. Oh, wouldn't that be nice. Parenting is a thankless job, and the only person that is able to show you appreciation, especially through these early years, is the person that helped you create that child. That's it.

You are the other parent's only real cheering squad. You are the only other person on this planet that knows what it's like to parent your child. You. So, if you have a partner, or ex-partner that picks up the slack, say thank you. Even if you don't hear it back. Say thank you for handling that conference because I couldn't get out of work. Thank you for taking them to get their braces adjusted. Thank you for picking up diapers while I was trapped inside with a vomiting toddler, and a baby that was wearing their last clean diaper. Thank you for sticking around and choosing to keep showing up. Thank you is so simple, but it's such a powerful, and motivating phase. Don't be stingy with it.

Last little tidbit on this subject, and then I really have to move on. I mean, I don't have to I suppose, but if I keep sitting her typing, this chapter will be 300 pages all by itself. Be respectful, you guys. Respect is worth its weight in gold. Be respectful to their face and be respectful when your children are in the house, or around in general. You notice I didn't just say when your kids are in earshot. Kids have bat ears when they hear you talking negatively about their other parent, so just don't do it. Let me tell you what you're saying to your kid when you talk about their other parent negatively. You're telling your kid there's something wrong with them. You're telling your kid you don't like them. You're telling your kid that they are somehow broken or damaged. No, I'm not crazy. I know you would never say those things to your child, but when you talk about their other parent in a negative way in front of them, or to them, you are talking about a part of your child. They will internalize that. Their mom or dad could be the worst parent ever. They could be in jail for doing terrible things, but you don't need to say anything negative about them. Give the facts and only facts, "Mom said she couldn't make it." Leave off the *again*, that I know you desperately want to attach to that sentence. "Dad said maybe next weekend." Just facts. No flourish, no excuses. Your child will figure out on their own, the truth about their other parent if they are inconsistent, or bad people in general. It is not your job to plant that seed, but it's also not your job to make excuses.

Be there for your child. Pick up the pieces if the other parent has an issue with following through. But don't make excuses for the other parent. Don't give them an easy out. If they just don't show up, without calling, just let them know that. "Mom must not be coming, bud." There's no need for name calling. No need for mumbles under your breath or venting to your child, or neighbor while your little one can hear you. If you need to, write in a journal. Call them all sorts of names on a piece of paper and then burn it (in a safe way). But whatever you do, don't let the words pass your lips while your little sponge is still awake. When they go to sleep, feel free to sit on your porch and quietly scream whisper into your phone while your sister tells you how much of a jerk the offending parent is. Co-parenting can be a challenge, but if we can remain respectful, appreciative, compromising, and communicate well, we will be on the path to a peaceful experience.

25

Houston, Do We Have a Problem?

This parenting gig is hard. I certainly understand, that it can be extremely difficult at times, and even more so if your child has special needs. But what about those parents that are struggling with the thought that their child might have an undiagnosed different need than other children? They may feel very confused and lost. They may be questioning every parenting decision they are making due to not knowing if their child is on par developmentally or not. They are feeling all alone, embarrassed, and out of sorts. Parents that are struggling with determining if your child has a disorder, or not, please do not feel like whatever is going on is your fault. It is hard to decipher at times what is normal and what is abnormal behavior, unless it is so abnormal that you just can't miss it.

My daughter was 13, before we got her diagnosis of Autism Spectrum Disorder. Back when she was diagnosed, it was called Asperger's. I knew something was off, but I just couldn't put my finger on it. Her behaviors were within the "normal" range, and she responded well to behavioral techniques mentioned in this book, so I really had no reason to think she had a major issue, so we just chalked it up to her being weird. Which, weird in our house, is sort of a requirement to live there, so it just didn't seem that strange to me. Here I am with a degree in child development, and I missed my child's diagnosis. Once she was diagnosed, all of the pieces started to fit together. When it comes to girls on the spectrum, they are often diagnosed later than boys. It could be because girls, even when on the spectrum, pick up more social cues than boys do, so they learn to "blend" a little better than boys. It could be that, girls are not displaying the more severe symptoms of having Autism Spectrum Disorder. I am honestly not sure, and any information I would have on the subject on why girls are diagnosed later than boys would be from my daughter's old psychologist, when she was explaining it to me.

We were lucky though, we moved to a very small town, and the teachers noticed something was going on. They paid attention to what was going on with the children academically, but also socially. So, it was her 7th grade teachers that said, "we notice that she doesn't like the loud noises of the bells." and "she just walks and sits near other students, she's not really interacting with them." They didn't say she was being bullied, but they noticed she had no friends, but stood and sat with the same group of girls, completely without interacting. They noticed her excessively picking at the small blonde hairs on her fingers, and hitting her hands together while answering a question, or in stressful situations, like state testing. These are things we didn't notice at home, because she was at home. We aren't giving out stressful tests, and we certainly aren't expecting her to chitchat with the girls in the hallway, because she's the only girl in the house, besides me, and she is just a quiet child. Her obsession with animals, and how she even knew what the word brachycephalic meant at the age of 6, just made her quirky. Her compulsion to draw 15 hours a day, even while completing homework, just made her an artist. Her inability to hold eye contact for more than 10 seconds at a time, made her shy. Her lack of social skill and social etiquette made her immature. Her aversion to meats and certain textured foods, made her a picky eater. It didn't make her Autistic. Autism wasn't even on my radar, because she had friends. She was smart. She wasn't lining up her toys or doing things in a repetitive manner. She was making eye contact and voicing her opinions. She was just immature. She was just shy. She was just quirky.

 I felt so alone, and so very stupid for missing something this big that was staring me in the face since she was a child. When she was a toddler, she didn't want to eat anything but macaroni and cheese, and we thought it was just because she was a toddler, but the texture of meat literally made her gag. As very young parents, we thought she was just being dramatic. When she didn't make eye contact, we gently held her face and told her she had to look at us when she was speaking to us, so we would know who she was talking to. When she told us all about dogs, and how long they stayed pregnant and what foods they couldn't eat at the age of 4, we told her how smart she was. None of this rang any bells. None of this made us think, as young parents that something could be going on. All of her milestones were made right on time, or early. We didn't know. I didn't get my degree in child development until she was graduating kindergarten. In fact, we graduated a month apart. Once I had my degree in hand, I thought something could be off. She was tested, and diagnosed with ADHD inattentive type at 7, but back then, girls having Autism was rare. So rare, that they really didn't test for it unless it was obvious they had overt characteristics of the diagnosis.

In hindsight, I know it was not my fault. I know I had no reason to feel stupid, but I can't help how I felt at the time. I can't help that in that moment the dreams I had for her altered, and I hurt my own feelings. It was also shortly after I had that pity party that I realized that I was imposing my own dreams on my child. Whether she had a diagnosis or not, didn't mean she was going to get married, go to college or whatever else I had planned out for her. She is her own person. My boys are their own people. Your children are their own people. We cannot impose our desires onto our children.

If you are in a situation where you are not sure if these behaviors are due to a developmental issue, or simply unruly behavior, my suggestion to you would be to keep an eye on it. If you have been consistently trying a specific behavior technique for weeks, before moving on to a new technique and there is still no improvement, seek professional help. Make sure everyone in the household is being just as consistent with the decided upon behavior modification techniques first. There are plenty of times where I see parents believing they are being consistent, when the other parent is not. This sends the child mixed messages, and they will act out accordingly. One parent doing one thing, and the other parent doing something else is basically the equivalent to neither parent being consistent on anything. If you aren't on the same page when it comes to parenting, your children will behave like they have little to no rules, even when they may have several.

If you know that you have been doing everything in your power to keep things consistent, and there are still behavior problems, then it's time for an evaluation. Sometimes we have to know when to tap out. Then there are times when behavior is not the issue, and there are developmental concerns, such as delays in speech or motor skills. These are areas that are a bit easier to spot because they are in your face symptoms, especially if your children are around others their age. If you notice these developmental issues, you should speak to your pediatrician, so they can begin the process of evaluating your child. The earlier things like this are detected, the better the results will be in the long run. Early intervention services are such a fabulous tool for parents to utilize. So, if you notice something is going on, or just "doesn't seem right," talk to your child's doctor. If they aren't taking you seriously, then get a second opinion. It's allowed. I know as women, especially, we are pre-wired to not question people in authority, but I am giving you full permission. If something isn't right with your child, and your doctor is not listening...get a second opinion. Go to a specialist, like a child psychologist or clinical social worker, and ask for an assessment. You got this mama!

26
Handy Dandy Tips and Tricks

So, you want to know my secrets huh? Well, too bad, I don't really have any. I mean, I'm lying, but you don't know that. My tips and tricks are really very practical. In fact, most of them are sprinkled throughout this book, but if you'd like them all in one place, then read this chapter. I'm going to answer your burning questions about how I do it all. As I mentioned before, I don't do it all. I just don't. You know what else I don't do? I don't feel bad about not doing it all. So, check your guilt at the door. Is my house clean at all times? I could literally laugh out loud at that question. Heck no.

My house contains four children, and five animals. It is not clean every day. I don't stress about it either, because when my kids are older, and have children of their own, they will not remember if our house was spotless all the time. What they will remember are the fun things we did.

They'll remember dance parties in the kitchen. They'll remember making "glerch" before it was called slime with added ingredients. They'll remember their mother making up the tallest tales, just to get them to giggle when they were teenagers and way too cool to hang out with me. They won't remember who did what chore, or how many times I mopped the floor this month. Do you remember that about your childhood? I sure don't.

Don't sweat the small stuff. Don't live in filth, but don't sweat the small stuff either. Speaking of small stuff, stop overburdening yourself with these planned activities. You are not a preschool. They do not have to move through the house in stations. Remember what I said about letting them be bored? Actually, do it. Let them be bored. Don't run yourself ragged trying to entertain your children. Your job is not to entertain them. Your job is to create good citizens. Nowhere in the world does it say that mom has to stand on her head and do kickflips on a longboard to make sure her kids never experience one millisecond of boredom. I'm honestly not sure where this notion came from, but it is damaging our fellow moms. You are not a jester. Play with them, but don't fall into the habit of placing their main source of entertainment on you. They're children. They turn sticks into light sabers, and Legos into rocket ships. Let them do that.

Wake up earlier than them. What? I know I sound off my rocker but hear me out. I wake up earlier than my children. I almost always did. There were a couple of years that I didn't wake up until it was time to wake them up, and my life felt chaotic and just overwhelming. If I can get up and moving an hour or two before them, I have time to drink my coffee in peace. In complete silence, y'all. Sometimes I just sit there in the dark with the over the sink light illuminating my shadow like I'm in some weird horror movie, just so I can sit in silence. No tv, no anything. I also have time to make breakfast if I want. I can make sure they get out of the door with a full belly instead of whatever they're going to get in the cafeteria that morning. It also gives me time to load the dishwasher or sweep the floor. The mornings give you a chance to start the day on your own terms. No one else's. By the time you need to wake up the kids, you've had a minimum of 20 minutes of silent bliss, straightened the house, and cooked breakfast. You're ready. You're ahead of the game. Your patience is long because you took care of yourself first. This leads me to my next tip.

Take care of you. You know how the flight attendants tell you to place the oxygen mask on your face before placing one on your child's face? Yeah, just like that. Take care of you. You are no good to anyone else, if you're drowning. You're no good to anyone else if you don't ask for help when needed. You're no good to anyone else if that's all you think you're good for, being good for other people. Your sole purpose in life is not just to care for others. You get to have help. You get to have some personal time. You get to still be you. Try not to forget that girl. Try not to let go of those dreams. Try not to give yourself the short end of the stick. You deserve all of the help and happiness that you're trying to produce for others in your life.

Get organized. Now listen here. On this part, you're going to do as I say and not as I do. I'm not talking about going Marie Kondo on your family, though it may help. I'm just saying have a system that works for you. Know where things are. If you don't have a place for things, create a place. If your house is unorganized, your life is unorganized. My organization skill is lacking in some areas more than others, but I do have a system that works for me. My important papers have a home, even if at times it's just the important paper pile, until I move it to the important paper file folders. Organizing will make cleaning so much faster and easier. It'll also make you feel accomplished. There are also some moms who have a side hustle of organizing other people's houses. If this step overwhelms you, hire them. Let this other mama come in and get your house in order. Take some stress off of your plate and put a little cash in her pocket. If you don't have enough money to hire someone, start slow and start at the Dollar Tree. They have a lot of organization items, for a fraction of the price that you would pay at a department store.

Make a plan. Plan for meals, and plan for who is doing what. Communicate these plans with the other adult in the house and the older children if they will be helping to share the load. Everyone in the home should have roles to play, not just you, mama. You should have help, and it comes in the form of your family. So, make the plan. Is your teens specialty pizza, well, on Fridays it's pizza night and Jake is taking the wheel. Does your husband make a killer meatloaf, slap that bad boy on the schedule for Tuesdays, and kick up your feet while he cooks. You know the person cooking dinner needs peace, so make that time the 30 minutes out of the day that the kids get to do an activity in their room or play outside with the non-busy parent. This is your house. Sit down with your partner and make a solid plan. Stick to it.

Use your inside voice. These kids drive you crazy sometimes. I know. Mine drive me up the wall too. Keep your cool and use your inside voice. The cool thing about using your inside voice is, it makes you feel better. It makes you keep your adrenaline in check, so you can think more clearly and express what you want to say. Plus using your inside voice allows your children to see that even when you're frustrated, or angry, you can still keep control of your faculties.

Practice daily gratitude. It is so easy to compare ourselves to others and think of all the things we are lacking. Sometimes we swim in our own negativity, simply because the water's warm there. Stop it. Stop it right now. I don't care that it's familiar. I don't care that it's warm and welcomes you with open arms. I don't care, that you've always done that. Stop. Swimming in your own negativity, only breeds more negativity. If you're only looking for the negative things in life, then you're only going to see the negative things in life, and you're going to miss out on all of the beautiful things your life has already in place. So, take a few minutes every morning or at the end of each day and practice gratitude. Think about all the good things that happened in your day. Something positive happened, even when it feels like it didn't. Did the sun shine just the right way? Did your little one come the first time you called? Did your lasagna turn out just the way you planned? Something good happened today. You just have to find it. Write the things you're thankful for down on a piece of paper or say them out loud to yourself in the shower. Whatever way you choose to practice gratitude is up to you, just do it daily. Once you get in the habit, your brain goes on autopilot looking for good things to report to yourself.

Don't stop dreaming. This one is so important to me. I want you to think about what you want out of life. What is it that you always wanted to do or be outside of your children? Got it? Now, say it out loud. Even if it's just a whisper. Say it out loud. Breathe a little life into that thing that's solely you. No one else can do that thing like you can do that thing. Imagine you doing the thing that you just pictured. How did that make you feel? Yeah, go after that. People get lost when they have children. They start going with the flow of their household, and slowly lose who they are. Maybe your dream was to always be a mom, and you've reached it, but what if it wasn't what you thought it would be? What if you still feel an internal pull to do something else? Would you ignore it, or take the steps to go after it? It's OK to admit that the life you envisioned isn't what you thought it would be. It's OK to say, I wanted to be a nurse, but now that I'm doing it, and I've been doing it for a while, I want to try something new. It's OK to say that as a mom, too, if you don't work outside of the house. Don't think I'm saying run away from your children. As much as we may want to do that from time to time, don't actually do it, but do dream as big as you did before you had those sweet babies. If you want to go back to school, go. If you want to start working on your own business while your little one naps, I'm rooting for you. If you want to quit your job as a corporate attorney and be a full time stay at home mom, go for it! Whatever your dream is. Whatever that little whisper was a few minutes ago, go after it.

Stop saying I'm sorry. There are so many times that women, especially say I'm sorry when they have absolutely nothing to apologize for. Let people own up to their own issues and mistakes. Don't you be the mommy martyr. Don't you apologize to keep the peace. Instead, say thank you. Replace I'm sorry with thank you. Does that sound weird? I'm sure it does but take that power back. You deserve to have some power too. Someone is upset with you, even though it's not your fault, don't apologize. Say thank you for letting me know you were upset. Say thank you for feeling comfortable enough to express your feelings. Don't say I'm sorry, unless you actually did something to feel sorry for. Rachel Hollis wrote a whole book about it, called *Girl, Stop Apologizing*. Her book isn't all about apologizing, it's about reaching your potential and living your best life. If you haven't read it, give it a go.

Build your tribe. If you don't already have a tribe, then it's time to build one. A small group of friends that understand your struggles, and by all accounts, you understand theirs, is sanity saving. Trading childcare, dinners, and playdates can be everything your mom heart needs. When my older kids were younger, my mom tribe was strong, and it took so much weight off of my shoulders. We had days where dinner would be cooked at one person's house and a family or two would come over for dinner, and then the next week it would be at someone else's house. We cooked together, traded childcare for date nights, and had laughs and cried over a bottle of wine after the kids went to sleep. So, if you don't have a mom tribe, or have outgrown yours for whatever reason, build yourself a new one. It can be challenging, but it's worth it.

Give yourself some grace. This is my final "tip" in this chapter, because it's the most important. I mentioned it earlier in the book, as I've mentioned a few of these other tips earlier in the book as well. This one is the most important because we are our own worst critics. We nag ourselves and beat ourselves up in a way that we wouldn't dare do to someone else. We would feel absolutely ashamed of ourselves if we spoke to other people or expected perfection from others like we do of ourselves. So, give yourself some grace. Cut yourself some slack. No one is perfect. No one. You will make mistakes, but mistakes can be corrected. You will say the wrong things, but we all do. Treat yourself kindly, and practice forgiveness with the person in the mirror.

Acknowledgements

I don't even know where to start with this, because it will make me cry. I guess the question is, do I want to cry now, or cry later, because the tears are going to come. Might as well rip the Band-Aid off. This year was a year of change for me, and it's mostly because my dad died. He was always one of my biggest supporters, so, thank you William. Thank you for believing in me, even when I was floundering around trying to figure out what I was going to do with my life. I didn't have it all figured out until you left this earthly home, but you were proud of me nonetheless. Thank you for stepping in to be my dad when you didn't have to be. Thank you for being my protective factor to make sure I didn't wind up living in a cardboard box. I don't know that I could say thank you enough for all of the things you did to make sure that I was OK, but I have a feeling you know what's on my heart even when I have a hard time putting it to paper.

Thank you to my mom. You have been my biggest cheerleader from the start of my life, and you constantly reminded me of the great things I could do, even when I felt like you were grossly exaggerating my abilities. Thank you for listening to me cry and doubt myself. Thank you for constantly building me back up when I beat myself down. Thank you for marrying William, and modeling together, what a happy functioning family looked like. Thank you for being proud of me and nurturing me well past childhood. Thank you for always being kind and showing me how to be a good parent.

To my favorite sister, Jasmine. I know you're my only sister, but even if you weren't, I'm sure you'd still be my favorite. Thank you for pushing me to finish a book. Thank you for never giving up on me even when I started and stopped more books than I can count. Thank you for letting me bounce ideas off of you, and being a listening ear when I was confused, or didn't think I could keep going. You have been a best friend for many years now, and I'm so glad I have you in my life.

To my brothers. Yeah, y'all get combined. I have too many of you. Rol, you continue to inspire me with your talent. I still tell people that there's nothing my brother can't do. No sport, no talent that he doesn't possess. You have such a kind spirit, and big heart, and I love when you laugh because it makes everyone's heart laugh too. My cheeks hurt when you're around. Jamar, you have always been my protector, and one of my biggest fans. You make me feel like I'm able to conquer the world. Will, you are the sweetest, and such a big part of why I do what I do. I love you guys! Thank you for always believing in any and everything I dedicate my time to trying to figure out. I couldn't have picked a better family.

To my husband. Thank you for putting up with my early mornings and distracted conversations while I was trying to finish this book. You have been such a big support for me, whether it was constantly encouraging me to finish my MSW program, or just rooting for me when I have these big ideas that will mean you have to pick up my slack. Your support means the world to me, and I'm so happy that I picked you to do life with.

To my kiddos. You guys are the best! I'm so very glad that of all the mommies in the universe, you somehow picked me. I know, I know, you didn't really pick me because that's not how babies work, but I like to believe you did. So there!

I love you all, and hope I continue to make you proud.

Made in the USA
Middletown, DE
16 January 2026